CORNWALL'S
TOP TEN

INTRODUCTION

This little book is a condensed version of Goldeneye's Cornwall Guidebook. Goldeneye have been publishing Cornwall Travel Guides in various formats for 35-years and this is the second time a Top 10 has been identified by us. Those chosen has not been done lightly. Some come immediately to the fore, others have aroused debate. In an Age when time is at a premium and when the modern traveller seeks only the best and is given to short breaks it seems an apposite moment to re-publish this book. The Top 10 are included on merit and merit alone. We gain no advertising revenue from those listed in this book. Many also feature in our On-Line Guide.

Cornwall is a County of great diversity, of strange customs and superstitions, of romantic legends and Arthurian myths. A County steeped in its own language, culture and, outlook. Remote, and cut off from the rest of Britain by the Tamar, the Cornish have developed a proud individuality and resilient independence. The close proximity to the Gulf Stream provides a warm and equable climate. The magnificent coastline, relentlessly shaped by the elements, with its contorted rocks, precipitous cliffs, deep estuaries, smugglers' coves, golden beaches and picturesque harbours, is unmatched elsewhere in England.

The landscape is haunted by countless landmarks of early man; Long Barrows, Quoits, Hill Forts and Stone Circles, and to put these into an historic perspective, the Neolithic Period gave place to the Bronze Age around 2000 BC, the Iron Age lasted from about 500 BC up to Roman times, the first 4 centuries AD.

The Cornish skyline has been shaped by the remains of chimneys and engine houses, and by ramshackle desolate buildings beside the road - the remains of a once prosperous tin and copper mining industry.

With few exceptions, Cornwall has been noted for the setting of architecture rather than architecture itself. However, there are fine examples of medieval fortresses and elegant country houses surrounded by spacious gardens, as well as an increasing number of more modern buildings; Truro College, the Tremough Campus at Penryn, and the RNLI Lifeboat Station at Trevose Head.

Whilst working on this book I looked at the range of environmentally conscious hotels, B&Bs, and dining pubs, not to mention the traditional artisans who work with natures' produce to create beautiful pieces of art. It occurred to me that many of the places I have selected have strong and positive environmental practices. Most of the eateries, from pubs to country house hotels use locally produced food with low food miles thereby supporting local producers and a lot of the places to stay focus their business on protecting their beautiful surroundings for generations to come. It is surely no surprise that the inhabitants of such a beautiful County as Cornwall would want to use its resources but use them in a way that prolongs them rather than depletes them. With nearly 300 miles of coastland virtually wrapping around the whole county, it is little wonder that so much of the area has turned to the sea for its influences. Here, the skills of the fisherman and the chef come to the fore. Given the natural austerity of the farmland in the area, Cornish farmers have worked with nature to farm the livestock and crops that work with the natural vagaries of the area.

So, in short, you can assume that most of the places featured in this book use local food producers even though I may not say so. And, although not all hotels can be considered eco-friendly, many B&Bs in this book are just that (as well as being super places to stay).

I believe Cornwall to be a truly magical holiday destination, whether you have a weekend or a week.

Whether you have a particular interest in surfing, gardens, history, or simple hedonism. There is no shortage of options for you. Take a deep breath of sea air, shrug off your working persona…I promise you'll feel better.

William Fricker
Penryn,
April 2019

Surfer's Sunset, Bude

Bodmin. The County town of Cornwall is positioned in the centre of the county, just off the busy A30. It is worth a stop-over to explore the interesting museums, and the C15 St Petroc, the largest Parish Church in the County. It does not have the chic shops of Truro or the dramatic locations of Falmouth and Penzance. It is a quiet, country town full of history. Witness the historic prison, scene of public executions until 1862, and Protector/Keeper of the Crown Jewels in WWI. The Information Centre is set in the old Court House where the ghosts and spirits of unlucky souls foundered. A grand start-off point for the Camel Trail. Indoor swimming pool. E/C W. (100/C1) bodmin.gov.uk

Bude. A seaside resort first developed by the Victorians that has witnessed, of late, much resurgence, in no small part due to the popularity of surfing and beach activities. The long, extensive beaches, just a short walk from the town centre, and those to the south and north of the town, are breathtaking. The coastline demands respect and has been the scene of many shipwrecks - 80 ships were foundered, or wrecked between 1824-74. The town abounds with the buzz of surf shops, surf hostels and cafés, and when the Low Pressure is in force the beaches are populated with black shadows, in summer, and winter. It is the most accessible of the Cornish surf resorts. Canal carnival and fete - August (third week). 'Blessing of the Sea' - Aug. E/C Th. Food & Drink: Temple Cornwall and Life's A Beach. (91/H2) bude.co.uk

Falmouth. This is one town where it is best to arrive by sea (like Venice) to fully appreciate its position, for it overlooks a superb natural harbour. You will then avoid the inevitable bottle-neck of traffic when you come to leave. If you do arrive by car, park by the harbour and walk up the narrow high street brimming with independents; galleries, organic foodies, tea rooms. Don't miss the Old High Street, the coolest place in town. The new university at Penryn Campus has brought youthful exuberance to the town and brisk business. The Phoenicians and Romans came here in search of tin, and in the late C16, Sir Walter Raleigh persuaded the Killigrew family to develop the harbour's potential, and for 200 years it became the centre of the Mail Packet Trade, smuggling and piracy. Today, it is a popular yachting centre and home to these cultural venues: Pendennis Castle*, Maritime Museum*, Art Gallery*, gardens*, cinema, 3-beaches. Regatta week - mid Aug. E/C W. Food & Drink: Provedore, Stones Bakery, The Ope, Star & Garter, Beerwolf, The Wheelhouse and Olivers. (102/A9)

Fowey. Pronounced Foy. Fowey is a chic and fashionable town of narrow streets and brightly coloured houses that overlooks another superb, natural harbour. A haven for yachtsmen, and a commercial seaport, and, an attractive option with many pubs, delis, restaurants, galleries and shops. Look out Padstow you have some serious competition! This was one of England's busiest towns in the Middle Ages, and home of the 'Fowey Gallants', a bunch of reckless and invincible pirates who raided French and Spanish shipping. Today, still a busy exporter of China Clay, for you may witness the large ships delivering their cargo to which appears out-of-sync in this holiday town. The Daphne Du Maurier Festival Society presents the annual Fowey Festival. Museum*, Aquarium*, Fishing trips and passenger ferry to Polruan. Royal Regatta & Carnival week - Aug (2/3 week). Food & Drink: Life Buoy Café, Ship Inn, Kittows, Sam's, Pinky Murphy's Café, Haverners Bar and Old Quay House Hotel. (100/E8)

Fowey

Blue Anchor, Helston

Helston. The market town for the Lizard Peninsula and venue for the Floral Dance held around the 8th May. Elegantly dressed couples dance through the streets to welcome the coming of Spring. The locals take the opportunity to sample unusual quantities of the Spingo brew in the Blue Anchor, and often miss their step on leaving. Beware of the open drains. Don't miss the sophisticated Georgian houses in Church and Coineagehall Street. Birthplace of Henry Trengrouse, inventor of the rocket lifesaving signals. Boating lake, CAST Studios*, Folk Museum*, Flambards *. Harvest Fair - Sept (Ist week). Food & Drink: CAST Café, Blue Anchor. (104/E2)

Newquay. We all have our opinions of Newquay, and whatever they are, you can not argue with the superb beaches that have established Newquay as Cornwall's foremost surfing centre, and destination for partying youth, where it gets its fair share of hen, and stag parties, and thus suffers the blight of many English towns for the unruly and anti-social behaviour. For all of that, billions of pounds of property development has, and is, taking place. Tacky, old hotels and guest houses are being pulled down and are making way for luxurious apartments, evident as you head towards Fistral. To the north and south, outside of the town, are the quieter beaches. It, thus

Fistral Beach, Newquay

has, all the facilities of a modern resort; indoor and outdoor pools, Zoo*, Blue Reef Aquarium*. Fishing/boat trips from Quay, and a proliferation of camp sites. Carnival week - end May/ early June. Airport at St Mawgan for flights to and from Dublin, Gatwick, Heathrow (new) , Leeds, Manchester, Scilly Isles to name a few. Food & Drink: Boathouse, Bush Pepper, Fish House, FSC Surf Diner and Jam Jar. (94/B5)

of seafood and local produce. It is worth walking away from the crowded harbour, and exploring the side streets, or heading out for the coastal footpath to the nearby beaches. The Camel Trail starts here, and you can hire a bike from one of the hirers located beside the car park at the bottom of the hill. Food & Drink: Ben's Crib Box Café, Bin Two, Rojanos, Prawn On The Lawn, No. 6 and Stein's. (92/D8)

Padstow Harbour

Padstow. A labyrinth of narrow alleyways, and picturesque houses, and a safe haven on the treacherous North Coast. May Day heralds the arrival of the Padstow Hobby Horse ('Obby 'Oss) who prances and dances the streets taunting young, and not so young, maidens. A celebration of spring fever, and the coming of summer. C16 Raleigh's Court House on South Quay. C15 church. Boat trips. Centre of fine cuisine with many restaurants, most notably Rick Stein's various enterprises. Some have labeled the town, Padstein. A little unfair. True, he may have dominated our TV screens for an Age, but his success has rippled out across Cornwall, and made this old county a destination for lovers

Penzance. A lively and busy town tempered by a lovely climate, for sub-tropical flowers grow in the Morrab Gardens and, at nearby, Trengwainton*. The Town Trail takes you to Chapel Street (where you will find exquisite shops, galleries and restaurants), and the Egyptian House, and to Market Jew Street, dominated by the Ionic columns of Market House, and the Statue of Sir Humphrey Davy, inventor of the miners' Davy lamp. Look out for the Floating Harbour, and the ship Scillonia, which will ferry you to the Isles of Scilly, and besides you can also book shark and deep sea fishing trips. Other attractions; the swimming pools (in & outdoor), Penlee House Museum*. West Cornwall Spring

The Harbour, St Ives

Show - late March. Food & Drink: Cornish Hen, Honey Pot, Navy Inn and The Shore. (107/H6)

St Ives. A labyrinth of narrow streets, whitewashed cottages, brightly coloured boats and sandy beaches so bright, piercing and clear you could be forgiven you believed you had arrived in a Mediterranean village. The light drew in the early painters in the C19 and C20 and the sea has a magical turquoise colour and today very much the southwest's centre for contemporary arts and crafts. Also, a centre for fine cuisine, especially locally-caught seafood. Its charm remains unaltered by the thousands who flock here. It is a special place worth exploring and, you never know, you may benefit from one of the art courses on offer. Barbara Hepworth Museum*, Leach Pottery*, Tate St Ives*. Music & Arts Festival - Sept. Food & Drink: Porthminster Café, Porthmeor Café, Allotment Deli, Digey Food Rooms, Seafood Café, Alba and The Tate. (107/K1)

Truro. This is Cornwall's Cathedral city, administrative centre, and the major shopping centre in the county, always a hustle and bustle. There are elegant and beautiful buildings of the Georgian and Regency period, and on Lemon Street, the Assembly Rooms of 1772, the Mansion House and Prince's House in Princes Street, and the Cathedral*, 1880- 1910. The City has seen much development of late with its multiple stores and offices and flats overlooking the river, and a wealth of contemporary architecture at Truro College, and with the new hospital buildings. Art Gallery & Museum*. Cinema. Food & Drink: Arts Café, Cornish Vegan, Old Grammar School, Thomas Daniell, Lemon Street Market, Cornish Food Box and Great Cornish Food Store beside Waitrose. (102/B4)

Walkway to Cathedral, Truro

SMALLER CENTRES

Camborne & Redruth. These two towns appear as one. Formerly Cornwall's great mining centre, and the hive of great endeavor, industry and skill. The birthplace of Richard Trevithick, 1771 - 1833 designer of the high-pressure steam pump which revolutionized mining, enabling water to be pumped out at great depths. Tin mining halted in the 1930s due to imports of cheap Malaysian tin. There are some handsome buildings to be seen and many pretty rows of terraced houses, which if up country, would be in great demand. Cinema. (98/D6)

Cawsand & Kingsand. Twin villages with narrow streets and colourful houses. Former C18 smuggling centre, and anchorage for Plymouth. Park in Kingsand and walk through to Cawsand, the prettier of the two, and stroll across to the ancient pilchard works. Plenty of pubs to savour – you may have found your true home? Fine walks along the coast to Cremyl Ferry. Food & Drink: Old Bakery Café, Old Boathouse and Devonport Inn. (87/J9)

Hayle. Formerly a small port and industrial centre. The foundries once made all the castings for every Cornish mine, and at nearby Copperhouse there were tin and copper smelting works. The 'Saltings' is a reserve for migratory birds. 3 miles of superb sand and Paradise Park*. (98/A7)

Marazion. Reputed to be the oldest town in Cornwall. Lies opposite St Michaels Mount* and thus the embarkation point for thousands who rarely venture into this village. The safe sandy beach, and children's playground are an added family attraction. Reputedly, Joseph of Arimathea traded here in tin. Classical galleried Methodist chapel built in 1862.

Many art galleries. Food & Drink: BCK Bistro, Copper Spoon and Godolphin Arms (for the view). (107/K6)

Lostwithiel. A charming town, and a great favourite of mine, often overlooked because travellers fail to drive off the main road into the side streets. The C13 capital of Cornwall and as the Stannary capital oversaw the administration of the medieval tin industry. Hence, the wonderful mix of architecture - the town is packed with beautiful buildings: C13 Duchy Palace on Quay Street, C13 Parish Church, C17 and C18 Georgian houses on Fore Street and C18 Guildhall. Not forgetting, the C13 bridge, and all is set amidst the beautiful Fowey Valley. Outside the town, up a steep hill, Restormel Castle*. May Making ceremony, 'Beating the Hounds' - May (1st Monday) Gala week - late July. Festival week - end of August. Regatta -Aug BH. E/C W. Food & Drink: Trewithen Restaurant and Calogero's. (100/D5)

St Agnes. A former mining community, hence the skyline is jagged with disused engine houses. There is an arty ambience to this corner of Cornwall, quite different from other parts, perhaps more akin to Penwith. The birthplace of John Opie in 1761, Cornwall's most famous painter who became a Fellow of the Royal Academy at 26 and who is buried in St Paul's Cathedral. Family resort and centre for dramatic coastal walks. Museum. Arts & Crafts Trail. This is one of my favourite areas in Cornwall. HQ of "Surfers Against Sewage" at Wheal Kitty Workshops, a great destination with Canteen, Finisterre (clothing company) and Open where you can shape your own surf board. Food & Drink: St Agnes Bakery, St Agnes

Hotel, The Taphouse, Driftwood Spars and Schooners. (97/B10)

St Austell. The proximity of first Heligan and then Eden has brought unheralded attention to this old brewing and route centre whose original prosperity came from the china clay industry. The hinterland is made up of white mountainous pyramids, man-made lakes and palm trees. All heady stuff. Within the town, the fine C15 perpendicular church, the Holy Trinity, the C18 coaching inn, the White Hart and a Georgian Quaker House of 1829 all toll for the town's historic fortunes. To savour the adventures of the town's former merchants make your way to Charlestown, and admire the tall ships in dock. (100/A8)

St Germans. This was Cornwall's Cathedral City until 1043, and you are in no doubt of this when you stand before the superb Norman doorway to the church of St Germanus*. Next door, Port Eliot, was for centuries the seat of the Eliot family who now hold the annual Literary and Music Festival. The St Germans or Lynher River estuary is one of the great natural secrets of Cornwall. Elephant Fayre - July (last W).Food & Drink: Rod & Line, Carew Arms. (86/E6)

Three Mermaids, St Agnes

St Just-in-Penwith. A handsome little town formerly a hectic mining centre with an imposing Doric-facaded Methodist church. The area is rich in prehistoric antiquities and rich in artists and craftsman (and many galleries*). By Bank Square, the amphitheatre 'Plain-an-Gwary'. Water sports festival, Priest's Cove – July. Food & Drink: Café Dog & Rabbit, The Cookbook and Kegan Tea shop. (106/C5)

Tintagel. The village is composed of a long and rather uninspiring high street peopled with tacky gift shops and tearooms which originally existed to service the pilgrims and visitors to Tintagel Castle. The setting is spectacular and strange and it is easy to fantasize about Merlin and magic. For remarkable views and a sense of Nature's violence take a walk onto the Island and around the Castle then out to the neighbouring outcrops: Barras Nose and Willapark particularly spectacular on a stormy day. This is the perfect place to immerse yourself in Arthurian legend as inspired by Geoffrey of Monmouth in the C12, and later by Tennyson's 'The Idylls of the King'. Summer Carnival. Visitor Centre. Food & Drink: Charlie's, Olive Garden and Port William Inn. (93/M2)

Wadebridge. A busy and feel-good market town that has seen much recent development; new shops, eateries and galleries have brought a buzz and liveliness to this old, sleepy town, and venue for the Royal Cornwall Show in June. Magnificent C15 bridge with 17 arches. Superb views from the New Bridge on the A39. Mid-point for cycling the Camel Trail. Cinema. E/C W. Food & Drink: Strong Adolfos (A39), Stepping Stone, Relish and Glasshouse. (93/H10)

Boscastle Harbour

Boscastle. An Attractive village within a steep valley leads down to a sinuous and dramatic harbour. A safe haven on a treacherous coastline, and despite this it remains an extremely difficult portal destination to navigate into (especially on a stormy night). More recently, featured in the national news following the horrific flooding on the 16th August 2004. Cars and caravans were swept into the sea. Houses and shops were destroyed. The Royal Naval helicopter squadron from Chivenor, North Devon was magnificent in their efforts to save life, and limb. There are two cafés down by the harbour. Food & Drink: National Trust Café, Napoleon Inn, The Wellington and Boscastle Farm Shop & Café. (90/A9)

Charlestown. There's a nostalgic atmosphere about this C18 port built by Charles Rashleigh. Still a busy exporter of china clay. Shipwreck and Heritage Museum*, Diving centre. Pottery. Often used as a location for TV/Films; Onedin Line, Longitude, Poldark, Rebecca and Rosemary Pilcher's novels. Food & Drink: Charlies, Rashleigh Arms and Wreckers. (100/A8)

Looe. You may think you are in a time-warp. Looe is still an active and scruffy Cornish fishing village with a bustling quay, tidal harbour and a web of narrow streets that provides an unforgettable tableaux of Cornish life. It still has the gift shops and smell of chip batter. But, you can buy fresh fish collected off the boats that morning or you can

Newlyn Reflection

walk the Looe Valley Line where a number of way-marked trails lead off along 8-miles of railway track from Looe to Liskeard. It's an embarkation point for deep-sea fishing trips. Fish market on East Looe Quay. Sub-Aqua Club. Food & Drink: Café Fleur, Sarah's Pasty shop, Pier Café, Simply Fish and Pengellys. (101/M8)

Mevagissey. One of Cornwall's most picturesque and unspoilt fishing villages. The fine inner and more recent outer Harbour have been at the centre of the town's history. The Phoenicians and Romans traded here. Shark fishing centre, World of Model Railways*, Galleries*, Folk Museum* and Feast of St Peter - June (last week). (103/L4)

Mousehole. Pronounced 'Mouzel'. The least spoilt of all Cornish fishing villages, and the author's favourite. Stone cottages huddle around the harbour facing east, sheltered from the prevailing winds. Wander the streets and discover art galleries and special eateries, and if in need of a rest, sit on the harbour wall and watch a time capsule of Cornish life pass you by. Originally called Port Enys when it was sacked and burnt down by Spanish privateers in 1595. More recently, memories still linger of the terrible tragedy that struck the village in December 1981 when the Penlee Lifeboat, the Solomon Browne and its 8-man crew perished in appalling weather. Fishing trips, carnival - Aug (2nd/3rd week). Galleries*. Food & Drink: The Old Coastguard Hotel, 2 Fore Street and Hole Foods Deli. (107/H8)

Newlyn. Home of Cornwall's largest fishing fleet where at day break the lively fish market is in full voice. The medieval quay is a delight. Like St Ives, a favourite haunt for artists - Edwardian painters came and left much work behind. Sadly, much of Newlyn was destroyed by Spanish Raiders in 1595 and by the Penzance Council in 1937 when 85% of the fisherman's cottages were

The Harbour, Charlestown

pulled down. Art Gallery*. Fresh fish and shell fish merchants, aplenty. The pubs tend to be patronised by thirsty trawlermen. If you can cope with that you may experience something new. Food & Drink: Tolcarne Inn, Jelberts Ice Cream, Mackerel Sky Seafood Bar, Newlyn Filmhouse Café, Italian Kitchen & The Swordfish. (107/G7)

Penryn. An attractive town with a picturesque steep main street and handsome Georgian houses is situated at the head of Penryn Creek. Granted a Charter in 1236, and thus a much older community than nearby, Falmouth. In the C17, England's busiest port after London. In the C19, the export of granite began, and has continued supplying New Scotland Yard, four London Bridges and the Fastnet Lighthouse. The home of the Penryn Campus, the new University and Art College buildings of the Universities of Falmouth & Exeter. Museum*. Town Fair - Aug BH W/E. Food & Drink: Muddy Beach Café, Stargazy Café, Earth & Water Deli, Origin Coffee and Thirsty Scholar. (99/M9)

Polperro. The quintessential and "Pretty As A Picture" idyll of a Cornish fishing village. It is yes picturesque for a timeless ambience pervades the narrow streets, pastel- shaded cottages and colourful harbour. It can be crowded during the day. Best

Porthleven Harbour

visited in the evening when most are dining. And, you can enjoy a pint at the Blue Peter Inn and if in luck listen to the Fisherman's Choir practicing. Model Village and tea/gift shops. Fishing trips and Regatta; mid-July. Food & Drink: Blue Peter Inn, The Wheelhouse, Museum Tearoom and Couch's. (101/J9)

Port Isaac. A charming little port; a steep street runs down to a little harbour, hazardous when a northerly wind blows. Lobster fishing centre. Trips for mackerel, pleasant inns and parking (charge) on beach at LT. Pottery. Fresh fish merchant. Location for the TV serial, Doc Martin, and the films Fisherman's Friend and Saving Grace. St Endellion Music Festival - Aug. Food & Drink: Ruby Tuesday Café, Golden Lion Inn, The Slipway, Port Gaverne Hotel and Restaurant Nathan Outlaw/Fish Kitchen. (93/H6)

Porthleven. Attractive harbour with shipbuilding yard, C19 Harbour House and imposing Wesleyan chapel c.1890. The vulnerable harbour faces south west and was built for the mining industry in 1811. A south-westerly gale in 1824 washed it away, to be later rebuilt in 1855, with lock gates. Serious Surf Break off the Harbour wall for the most determined surfer. Food & Drink: Nauti But Ice Café, Kota, Seadrift Kitchen Café and Ship Inn. (104/C3)

VILLAGES OF INTEREST

Altarnun

Altarnun. A bit off the beaten track but when all is said it is a charming linear village with a superb C16 church*, the 'Cathedral of the Moors' and worthy of your attention. Packhorse bridge. Rising Sun Inn. (84/K4)

Cadgwith. Thatched cottages of green serpentine rock and boats beached on the shingle cove create a romantic scene. Haunt of artists. Superb coastal scenery. Food & Drink: Café, Cadgwith Cove Inn and Fish shop. (105/H9)

Calstock. A sprawling, former river port on the river Tamar. The thickly wooded river bank has an abundance of fruit growing and provides splendid colour in Spring. The 12-arch viaduct is a memorable sight, too. Numerous disused mining chimneys and engine houses continue to haunt the landscape. (83/J10)

Coverack. A charming, picturesque old fishing village and former smuggling centre given to bucket and spade holidays. Small harbour. Food & Drink: Fish'nchips in Old Lifeboat Station. (105/L7)

Lamorna. A pretty village beside a wooded valley and since the Newlyn School, a favourite of artists and craftsmen. Summer craft exhibitions. Small jetty. Food & Drink: Café at Cove, Lamorna Wink Inn. (106/F9)

Morwenstow. Famous for Richard Stephen Hawker (1803-75) the eccentric and original vicar-poet and originator of harvest festivals. A compassionate man, he would stalk the wild coast in beaver hat, fisherman's long boots and yellow cloak in search of shipwrecked sailors. Many are buried in his churchyard. And, to stir (or wake) his congregation he would often dress up as a mermaid. Rectory Tearooms, opposite the church. Bush Inn. (88/B7)

Mullion. A busy village, and centre for much of the Lizard Peninsula. There is a splendid church, some pubs and cafés, an active cricket club and an award-winning school. The one-way system will draw you in and dismiss you but first bear left and make your way down to the Cove. The beaches close to: Poldhu and Polurrian are often empty but for a local dog walker. (104/F7)

VILLAGES OF INTEREST

Polruan. An attractive village with a busy boatyard. The main street plunges almost vertically to the small quay. Cars not encouraged. Superb views from the hill top car park. Worth the excitement of taking the pedestrian ferry to and from Fowey. The coastal walks are quite flat and re-assuring. Food & Drink: Lugger Inn. and Crumpets Teashop. (100/F9)

St Mawes. When the sun shines this village takes on a mediterranean air. It is popular with yachtsmen and their friends. It is the main centre for the beautiful Roseland Peninsula and home to the Hotel Tresanton and the Idle Rocks both set in enviable positions. Castle*. Food & Drink: Café Chandlers, Bakery, Hotel Tresanton, The Idle Rocks, St Mawes Hotel and Victory Inn. (102/B9)

Saltash. Most will rush past this little port and forget about it. An inspection of I K Brunel's bridge may be the exception to your rule, and you will be rewarded with chains of parabolas. The steep streets descend to the Tamar estuary. May Fair – 1st week. Regatta – June 3rd week. (87/H5)

St Mawes Castle

Sennen Cove. This isolated and independent community have for years made a precarious living from the sea. The old Lifeboat Station proud of a heroic history was established in 1853. The stone pier in 1905. Whitewashed cottages and the Round House Gallery* line the front. It is a popular surfing centre. Look out for the Celtic Cross in the car park. A visit to this shrine may improve your turns and barrels. Fishing trips. Food & Drink: Little BO Café, Surf Beach Bar and Old Success Inn. (106/A8)

Overlooking Cadgwith

High Tide, Bedruthan Steps

Cornwall is perhaps best known for its coastline and the multitude of beaches that pepper it. Nowhere in England is there such a quantity and variety of beaches – from wide, flat and open windswept beaches akin to many in the Southern Hemisphere, to tiny rocky coves with caves and imposing cliffs. Whether you want a safe place to visit with your family, somewhere to paddle in the shallows and eat ice cream, or if you want the rawness of nature to take your breath away, there are plenty of choices.

Bedruthan Steps, Nr Newquay. One of Cornwall's most dramatic beaches with a series of rock stacks crossing it which legend says were built by a giant named Bedruthan, who used them as stepping stones to traverse the bay. If you can negotiate the access which is via a very steep slippery staircase, you reach firm golden sands with massive rocks and caves. Tearoom. (94/C1)

Daymer Bay, Nr Rock. Popular family beach – ideal for young children due to its firm golden sands and sheltered position. Café. (92/E7)

Fistral, Newquay. This is the most popular surf beach in Cornwall and the clarity of the turquoise water is unparalleled. There are wide sands even at high tide and cafés for snacks to sustain you while you people and surf watch. (94/A5)

Kynance Cove, Nr Lizard. At low tide there are white sands and good bathing (in summer) as well

Bude Sandy Mouth

as serpentine rocks shaped over centuries by the rushing tides. At high tide it is too dangerous to swim but you can listen to the roaring noise of blow-holes and watch the violence of nature up close and personal. Get there early at low tide in summer and you could believe you were on a desert island. Café. (104/F9)

Perran Sands, Perranporth. The glorious 3-miles of sand has made this beach into the most visited beach in Cornwall - popular with dog owners, surfers and holiday makers.

Porthcurno, Nr Sennen. This is a white shell sand beach washed by turquoise sea and surrounded by high granite cliffs - a place of real beauty. Naturist section. (106/C10)

Porthleven Sands, Nr Helston. The steep shelving beach has a strong undertow and swimming is not encouraged making it less suitable for families. Ideal for a brisk walk across the four miles of sands – blowing away the cobwebs and enjoying the fantastic views across to Mounts Bay. (104/D4)

Porthmeor, St Ives. Just one of St Ives fabulous town beaches which is well served by local eateries and overlooked by Tate St Ives. Wide flat sands at low tide and popular with all. Café. (107/K1)

Sandy Mouth, Nr Kilkhampton. Expansive beach with swift currents and strong rip tides making it popular with surfers. Fabulous rock formations that glow at dusk. Firm sands and rock pools at low tide. Café. (88/B9)

Trebarwith Strand, Nr Tintagel. Extraordinary rock formations at the head of the beach. Very attractive at dusk when the setting sun hits the surrounding cliffs. (84/B1)

Watergate Bay, Nr Newquay. One of the few beaches in Cornwall that you can see from the road. It affords fantastic vistas even when you're just driving by. Very popular for extreme sports, therefore good for people and surf watching. Café. (94/B4)

Porthcurno Rocks

Rinsey Beach, Praa Sands

Chapel Porth. This has been described as a classy, fast and a hollow beach break. The sands are expansive indeed spacious at Low Tide but when the tide returns it comes at a rush. The currents are strong along this coast. Small National Trust car park at the bottom of a steep descent. Popular local beach break with folk from Wheal Kitty. Café/WC's. (99/G1)

Fistral, Newquay. This is the business. A consistent beach break and hence the most popular surf beach in Cornwall renowned for the clarity of the turquoise water. The surf can reach epic dimensions. It breaks Right with hollows at low tides. The North Side is usually bigger than South Fistral. There are wide sands even at High Tide and cafés to sustain you while you regain your stamina. Surf School. (94/A5)

Gwithian. Within the arc of St Ives Bay and protected. Hence, its popularity with beginners. The peaks are suitable for novices. Surf Academy and camping nearby. Some great cafés for nourishment. The High Tide can cut you off, so beware! (98/A5)

Praa Sands. A mile of golden sands and a popular beach with café on North End. The North End is protected from westerly winds and may produce a fast Right break. It can be another classy, tubular break and very busy. The East end at Hendra can create hazardous rips in a big swell but parking is tricky. (104/A1)

Sennen. This is the Holy Grail. Superb, consistent surf breaks just roll out shifting peaks and strong rips within a turquoise paradigm. The sea quality can rarely be bettered and can be overcrowded in summer. Surf School. Café. Camping nearby. (106/B8)

Female Surfer

Sennen Cove, Harbour Wall, Cornwall

Polzeath (Hayle Bay). This is a spacious beach ideal for families and novices. Its a popular slow beach break picking up most swells and can get crowded. There's a Right-hand wave off Pentire Point which creates big swells. Surf School and hire. Cafés. Ample parking. (92/E6)

Porthmeor, St Ives. This beach creates heavy fast surf and strong currents. There are fine peaks from a south-south westerly. The sands are spacious at Low Tide and popular. Night surfing is the ultimate in cool. A Dawny surf delivers a spectacle of iridescent delights. Surf School. Café. (107/K1)

Porthleven. This wave has the hot ticket to Nirvana! It can barrel like no other. An awesome break only for the experienced. The squeamish best stay at home. Technically, the reef lies on the west side of the harbour channel. At Low Tide its hollow, dangerous and kicks like a mule. Strong rips. (104/D4)

Perran Sands, Perranporth. This is a vast stretch of sand backed by dunes. The Rights peel off at the North End. Good at mid-tide with long rides. Lefts break off

Godrevy Island Lighthouse

the Headland. Beware of strong tidal flow. Great café. (97/D8)

Watergate Bay, Nr Newquay. One of the few beaches in Cornwall that you can see from the road. It affords fantastic vistas even when you're just driving by. Very popular for extreme sports (kite surfing) therefore great for people watching. Surf shop, surf school, bistro, bar and hotel. A long beach break popular with novices and Newquay locals. (94/B4)

Gateway to Helford View

We estimate that the average walker will achieve between 1.5 and 2 miles per hour. More like 1.5 miles. This takes into consideration time to admire the view, take photos and rest one's weary limbs. The super fit may well achieve 4 miles per hour. Much of the coastal footpath has steep descents and ascents so please be modest with your ambitions. Five hours of walking will be enough for most people. Best to walk in 4s and arrange transport at your journeys end or charge your smartphone and arrange a taxi.

Marsland Mouth to Bude: Approx. 19 miles. A remote and wild coastline; the rocks, razor sharp and contorted, the pathway hard going, yet exhilarating and rewarding. Rest at Morwenstow* and visit the church* and tearoom or Inn. Onwards, passing Parson Hawker's Hut and two miles on, the white satellite dish aerials of GCHQ at Cleave Camp, then into Duckpool where a path leads up to the Coombe Valley Nature Trail*. At low tide one can follow the sands to Bude or take the cliff top path. (88/B6)

Bude to Boscastle Harbour: Approx. 15 miles. Up to Compass Point for extensive views northwards. The path overlooks reefs, buttresses and pinnacles. Easy going to Widemouth Sands. Through car park, up Penhalt Cliff to Millook Haven with cliffs of contorted slate. Rough ascent to Dizzard Point (500ft), prone to landsliding, then onto veined and contorted rock forms of Pencannow Point. Easy descent to the fine sands of Crackington Haven, café. Hard going up to Cambeak - views from Hartland Point to Trevose Head. Climbing beside further landslipped sections, to pass jagged cliffs and The Strangles (beach) scene of many shipwrecks to High Cliff at 731ft the highest cliff in Cornwall (although slumping has created a massive sloping undercliff so it lacks the drama of a precipice) and supposedly a favourite courting and riding spot for Thomas Hardy and his first wife, Emma Gifford. Then to Beeny Cliff the only headland carved from Chert, a tough black flint-like rock and often below basking seals. Along to

Pentaragon Waterfall which falls 100ft down a deep chasm. And, the respite of Boscastle Harbour* for refreshments via Penally Point, and the tortuous harbour entrance. (91/G2)

Boscastle Harbour to Port Isaac: Approx. 12 miles.

The cliff walk to Tintagel along springy turf with spectacular views seaward to jagged rocks is quite superb. Worth a diversion inland to visit Rocky Valley and St Nectan's Kieve*, tearoom, a 40ft waterfall and ancient hermitage. Returning to the coast path. Offshore, Lye Rock once a renowned puffin colony - now the cliffs are nesting sites for fulmars, guillemots, razorbills and shags. The landscape is wild and remote, a place of legend and the romantic setting for the C13 Tintagel Castle* and the mass of older remains on Tintagel Island. On leaving the castle ruins the path climbs sharply to the cliff top church of St Materiana guardian of many shipwrecked sailors. Along Glebe Cliff past numerous old slate quarries to Trebarwith Strand* and café. A lovely beach to freshen up before the switchback path to Port Isaac*. (90/A9)

Padstow to Newquay: Approx. 16 miles.

A coastline dotted with superb sandy beaches and pounded by the mighty Atlantic rollers but best appreciated out of season. Splendid views at Stepper Point then on past caves and sheer cliffs at Butter Hole and Pepper Hole. The path hugs the coastline passing by campsites and beaches ideal for a quick dip. Look out for the emerald waters of Mother Ivey. The coastline is peppered with stacks and islands none more spectacular than at Bedruthan Steps* and NT café. Where legend has it that these stacks were used as stepping stones by the Cornish giant Bedruthan. Walk the clifftops in summer and bathe in the carpets of wild flowers that fill the air with the scent of burnet rose and gorse. Reaching Stem Point it's possible to walk the sands to Newquay at low tide; alternatively the headland path is easy going. (92/E8)

St Ives to Land's End: Approx. 22 miles.

Considered to be the finest stretch of all: wild, rugged and besieged, relentlessly by the elements. The path is lonely and remote. Up and down, up and down and at times hard going as it follows the cliff edge and clifftop.

RNLI Trevose Head

Cliffs, Land's End

Seals laze on the Carracks. A blow hole roars below Zennor Head. It's worth a detour to Zennor for refreshments and to meet the Mermaid in the church. On to Gurnard's Head (great hostelry), sphinx-like with great views, and now you are entering the heart of tin mining country, so beware of unprotected mine shafts. The cliffs between St Ives and Pendeen may glitter with minerals. Hereabouts, paths criss-cross in all directions, and there's much to interest the industrial archaeologist especially at Geevor, Levant and Botallack. Following the clifftops Cape Cornwall appears marked by a lonely stack, the remains of a mine abandoned in the 1870s. The cliff drops to Aire Point and ahead lies the thunderous breakers and dedicated surfers of Whitesand Bay. Café. And now the well worn path to Land's End. This is a sad case of where commercialism has ruined the natural landscape. It is obvious that if you look around at the appalling state of the footpaths you will surmise that the caretakers of this promontory have little regard for its future. As the old proverb puts it: "We do not inherit the earth from our ancestors, we borrow it from our children", or as Henry Ford so gallantly explained: "A business that makes nothing but money is a poor business." From the coastal footpath the natural landscape is indeed a sight to behold. There are dramatic cliffs and rock falls and when the light is exacting the sunsets can be magnificent. (107/K1)

Land's End to Mousehole: Approx. 15 miles. Yet, another superb stretch of coastline - precipitous cliffs, great blocks of granite, sandy coves and

Land's End Promontory

Lizard Point & Lifeboat Station

minute valleys with sub-tropical vegetation. Spectacular rock formations to Gwennap Head, equally as wild a headland as Land's End. Here are great, gnarled, granite boulders, cracked and sculpted by the elements; a popular place for climbers and below a haunt for seals. There are two paths: the first follows every cranny and contour, the second cuts off along the headlands for a wonderfully invigorating walk. Down into tiny Porthgwarra and on up to St Levan's Well above the little cove of Porthchapel. Then along to Porthcurno passing the famous Minack Theatre*; below an improbably turquoise sea and the outline of Logan's Rock. On around the dramatic granite columns of Treen Cliff, and then by Cribba Head, to the tiny fishing cove of Penberth. Along clifftops to Lamorna Cove and café, a favourite spot for artists. The path continues along the clifftop until Mousehole*. (106/A9)

Porthleven to Lizard: Approx. 13 miles. Interesting coastal path; craggy cliffs and splendid sandy beaches. The path follows cliff edge to Loe Bar*, Gunwalloe and Church Cove where apparently buried treasure is hidden. Onto the caves, arches and black rocks of Mullion Cove. Fine walking on clifftops around Vellan Head and past breathtaking precipices, to Pigeon Ogo, a vast amphitheatre of rock. The crowning glory is Kynance Cove, a spectacle of swirling currents (at HT), whooshing blow holes and wild-shaped serpentine rocks. Great bathing at LT and a, eco café. Then on along the well-trod path to Britain's most southerly point, Lizard Point. Caves and caverns about Polpeor Cove. East is the Lion's Den, a large collapsed sea-cave, a sudden vast hole in the cliff turf. Café. (104/C3)

Lizard to Falmouth: Approx. 26 miles. The east side of the peninsula is less rugged, the slopes are gentler, the landscape becomes more hospitable as one travels northward. First, you pass pretty Church Cove, and along the clifftop to the Devil's Frying Pan, a larger version of the Lion's

THE COASTAL FOOTPATH

Kynance

Den that roars when the easterlies blow. Through thatched Cadgwith to Kennack Sands where the path is easy-going, hugging the cliff edge and almost at sea level from Coverack to Lowland Point, scene of an Ice Age 'Raised Beach'. Offshore, at low tide 'The Manacles' are visible, a treacherous reef that has caused the death of more than 400 drowned sailors. Many lie buried (and forgotten) in St Keverne's churchyard. The 60ft spire of the church serves as a daymark for sailors and fishermen. At Godrevy Cove, the path turns inland to Rosenithon and Porthoustock to avoid quarries, returning to the coast at Porthallow - Fat Apple Café. A peaceful stretch to Gillan Harbour, possible to wade the creek at low tide or continue to bridge crossing the head of the creek at Carne. Through tangled woods to Helford village (Inn) and ferry across Helford estuary which runs from Easter to end of October to either Helford Passage or the beach at Durgan. From here the path passes Mawnan Old Church and along the clifftops to Falmouth. (105/G10)

Par Sands to Looe: Approx. 18 miles.
Lovely walk through pretty Polkerris, café, then up to the impressive cliffs of Gribbin Head (224ft) and an 84ft landmark erected by Trinity House in the 1820s. Fine views from the Lizard to Rame Head. At Polridmouth, sub-tropical flora and on up the path with good views of Fowey Harbour. Passing near the remains of St Catherine's Castle. Follow the road into Fowey where there is a regular ferry to Polruan. Then six miles of magnificent lonely clifftop walking to Polperro. Inland grazed fields and gentler contours, but the coast path is steep and hard-going. Polperro* must be explored, then along a well maintained path following the cliff edge to Looe. (100/C8)

Looe to Cremyll: Approx. 21 miles.
Soon to leave Cornwall's rugged coastline; Battern Cliffs (450ft), the highest cliffs in South Cornwall remind one of the dramas left behind. Past the little harbour of Portwrinkle, the path hugs the cliff edge and you can now walk through the M.O.D. ranges at Tregantle except during firing when you will be re-routed inland. Around the great sweep of Whitsand Bay to Rame Head with views of Plymouth Sound beyond. Along to the twin villages of Kingsand and Cawsand, passing Mount Edgcumbe and to Cremyll Ferry which has carried passengers across the Tamar since the C13. And, now for a pint or two of ale – or maybe a foot massage? You deserve it! (101/M8)

Porthcurno

Beach Hut, Watergate Bay ss

Beach Hut, Watergate Bay.
This is a child/family friendly café that provides fresh, simply cooked food when you need it most. And, when the last thing you want to do is cook for the family after a day in the surf. Fish and burgers feature, strongly. Daily Specials. Open from 8.30 till late. 01637 860877 (94/C4) watergatebay.co.uk

Fifteen Cornwall, Watergate Bay. Another success story for Jamie Oliver who helped set up Foundation Cornwall (Charity for Disadvantaged Children). Breakfast (first come, first served), lunch and dinner (require booking) served 7 days a week. The views are stupendous. The food, as you'd expect, is high quality. 01637 86100 (94/C4) fifteencornwall.co.uk

Godrevy Beach Café, Godrevy Towans. Serves breakfast, lunch and dinner. Choose from organic cakes, take-aways and barbecues. Sunset views from the decking area on stilts. Open from 10, all week. 01736 757999 (98/B5)

Hidden Hut, Porthcurnick Beach. It is amazing that a small, rustic, outdoor beach café with access via the coast path should host Feast Nights - that are now over-subscribed with 30,000 on their email list for a mere 150 covers to fill. Open daily for breakfast, lunch and tea in the season. Cash only. Connected to: Tatams Stonebaked. These converted loos provide fresh coffee, pastries, pizzas and fine views of Portscatho's beach. Open daily in season. 01872 581894 (102/D8) hiddenhut.co.uk

Life's A Beach, Summerleaze Beach, Bude. Bistro offers all types of food, from locally caught fish to burgers and pizzas. In a breathtaking position to capture the sunset at day's end. Open daily in season. 01288 355222 (91/G1) lifesabeach.info

Muddy Beach Café, Jubilee Wharf, Penryn. In grand position overlooking the estuary and boats at work and play. Opens at 9.30. 01326 374424 (99/L9) muddybeach.com

Nauti But Ice, Porthleven. Café serving amazing breakfasts, homemade cakes, baps, pastries and Cornish coffee. You can sit al fresco and admire the passersby, or just relax and enjoy the day. Open daily. Next door, Takeaways. 01326 573747 (104/C3)

Hidden Hut ss

Sea Spray, Fistral Beach, Newquay. Set on the rocks of Fistral Beach with a fine view of the surf and breaks breakfast lunch and dinner is served. All day coffees and teas. 01637 850793 (94/A5) seasprayfi-stral.co.uk

Sunset Surf (Surfer's Café/Bar), Gwithian Towans. A fun family-friendly hang-out, great food and facilities. Surf school and hire. Open daily from 10 for breakfast. 01736 752575 (98/A5) sunset-surf.com

Surf Beach Bar, Sennen Cove. A view of sand, sea and surf to die for and an eclectic decor of wood, glass and massive artworks. Burgers, pizzas and ciabattas served all day from the bar. 01736 871191 (106/B8) surfbeachbar.co.uk

You May Also Like to Consider:

The View Restaurant, Trenninow Cliff Road, Rame Peninsula. Your first stop, and no better introduction to Cornwall. Classic French food with English produce. Child and Veggie friendly. Open for lunch and dinner. T 01752 822345 (87/H9) theview-restaurant.co.uk

The Watering Hole, Perranporth. Actually situated on the sand, backed by dunes and fronted by the sea. A great view if you can see past the basting hoards on the beach on sunny days. Feels like a little slice of Oz. 01872 572888 (97/C9)

Waterfront Sandbar Café/Deli, Polzeath. Overlooks the beach in enviable position. Opens for late breakfast/brunch at 10. Al fresco lunches and evening meals. Style more bistro, than restaurant. Proudly serves local produce where possible. Open daily in season. 01208 862333 (92/F6) waterfront-polzeath.co.uk

The Waterfront, Polzeath ss

TOWN CAFÉS

Arts Café, 25 River Street, Truro. Set to the right of the Royal Cornwall Museum where in summer the pleasure can be eating al fresco, for the food is wholesome and the ambience lends itself to combing the daily papers and the art books on sale. In winter, a log burner warms your cockles and a hot drink and toasted panini will soothe your weary brow. 01872 240567 (102/B4) truroartscompany.co.uk

BCK Bistro & Bottle Shop, Marazion. Ben Prior is a chef who understands about the customers needs; value-for-money and hospitality. Here you have an unpretentious little bistro serving great food, and if required, accompanied by nectar in the form of viticultural delights. Open Tu-Sa from 12-1.30, 5.30-8.30. 01736 719200 (107/K6) benscornishkitchen.com

Café Dog & Rabbit, North Row, St Just. When its open this café is the place to eat, drink and relax after seeking out art and trekking the coast path. Arty and funky as well as providing nourishing fayre. Open June-Sept W-Su 9-4. 01736 449811 (106/C5)

CAST, 3 Penrose Street, Helston. The breakfast cooked by their French chef was something else; poached eggs and chorizo on sourdough. So good, I returned for lunch, then dinner. Events. Open Tu-Su 10-9 for breakfast, lunch and dinner. 01326 569267 (104/E2) c-a-s-t.org.uk

Cornish Vegan, 15 Kenwyn Street, Truro. A popular lunch venue; homemade buddha bowls, jackfruit sandwiches, burgers, vegan fish & chips, 'chickin' and sausages, cream teas and cakes to die for. Pretty Mediterranean garden. Dogs welcome. Indeed, it is also where carnivores can be surprised, learn and be nourished that there are alternatives to their daily diet. Open Tu-Sa 10-4. 01872 271540 (102/B4) thecornishvegan.com

Digey Food Room, 6 The Digey, St Ives. St Ives can be an exhausting place to visit; the crowds, the sea air, the mediterranean light, all bring on a thirst and an appetite and a need to sit down and rest with a cuppa. Herewith, a classy café/deli (and luxury food store) that serves all-day breakfast, soups, light lunches and a Cornish Cream Tea. Vegan/gluten food is an option, too. Open M-Sa 9-5. 01736 799600 (107/K1) digeyfoodroom.co.uk

Honey Pot, 5 Parade Street, Penzance. A café has been in this Art-Deco build for 100-years. Daily specials, exceptional soups, panninis, coffee and cakes, all with a flourish. You just can't go wrong here. Open M-Sa 10-6, lunch 12-late. 01736 368686 (107/H6)

Mackerel Sky Seafood Bar, New Road, Newlyn. As you walk, trawl the streets of Newlyn, perhaps visiting various art galleries or admiring the trawlers beside the docks, you will amass a mighty appetite for seafood (unless you are a Vegan) and there is no better place to drop into than this roadside café. On the menu is fresh seafood: scallops, mussels, lobster bake, fish and chips for lunch and dinner. Open daily March to October (inclusive) 12-3, 5.30-9. No bookings. (107/G7)

Mackerel Sky, Newlyn ss

Strong Adolfos Café ss

Mowhay Café & Restaurant, Trebetherick. Great place to stop for coffee, lunch or evening meal. Always interesting arts and crafts for sale. Open daily in season. 01208 863660 (92/E7)

Potager Garden & Glasshouse, Constantine. This is a "Find" that emerged from a bramble-filled wilderness. Only the finest ingredients are cooked with and it tastes so, so good. A treat. Craft studios. Open F, W/Es & BHs 10-5. 01326 341258 (105/H1) potagergarden.org

You May Also Like to Consider:

Provedore, 43 Trelawney Road, Falmouth. It's small, rustic, always ahead of the game. A basic café that started as a deli and through acute demand evolved into this modest café in the mornings turning into a restaurant serving South Asian/Pacific food in the evenings.. Open Tu-Sa 8.30-3.30, (& Th- Sa) 6.30-10. No bookings. 01326 314888 (99/M10) provedore.co.uk

Rick Stein's Café, 10 Middle St., Padstow. Light lunches, coffees, pastries and a reasonably priced three-course dinner each evening from Mr Padstein's acolytes. (92/E8)

Scarlet Wines, Old Forge, Griggs Quay, Hayle. Exhausted after belting down the A30? Stop off here for some nourishment and ogle at their gins, wines and cheeses. Perhaps, a strong cuppa to revive you. Feast Nights. Open daily from 9 for breakfast, lunch and dinner. Kids menu. Opposite the entrance to the Railway Station 01736 753696 (107/L3) scarlet-wines.co.uk

Stones Bakery, Old High Street, Falmouth. The town's finest bakery and coffee shop serving artisan bread, homemade cakes, pizzas and savoury tarts baked on the premises. Open M-Sa from 8.30. 07791 003183 (99/M10) stonesbakery.co.uk

Strong Adolfos, Hawksfield, Atlantic Highway. This café is a great destination for lovers of a supreme English Breakfast, Scandinavian cakes and various coffees/hot chocs. All served with a smile. Next door, the Natural Store at The Arc, Circle Contemporary Art Gallery, Finisterre Clothing and Goose Shed (bric-a-brac galore), and lots more. Open daily. 01208 816899 (92/F10) strongadolfos.com

Temple Cornwall, Granville Terrace, Bude. An obsession with design and the delicacies of life are what drives this new eatery and clothes emporium. It has to be organic and there will a choice of vegan/vegetarian as well as brunch, chicken and meat dishes. Opens at 10 for brunch. Open evenings, too. 01288 354739 (91/H2) templecornwall.com

Woods Café, Cardinham Woods, Bodmin. Treat yourself to daily baked cakes and savouries, delectable home-made food before or after your walk/cycle ride. Log fires in winter, Al fresco in summer, child and dog friendly. Open daily 10-4.30. Holiday Flat to let. 01208 78111 (100/E1) woodscafecorn-wall.co.uk

St Kew Inn ss

Cornish Arms, St Merryn. This pub is now part of the Rick Stein and St Austell Brewery empires. During the renovation of this old pub I couldn't help noticing the number and enormous size of the septic tanks being lowered into the ground. The owners planned for volume sales and I believe achieve it. The food offered is simple British pub menu; real beef burgers, mussels, chips and scampi in a basket. Beer garden. No reservations. Visit the Church, opposite. (92/C9) rickstein.com/The-Cornish-Arms

Carew Arms, Antony. A worthy destination for those seeking a pub, farm shop and café where your culinary expectations will be fulfilled. The chefs have a track record to impress the most precious of food junkies. 01752 814440 (87/G7) carewarms.co.uk

Ferry Boat Inn, Helford Passage. The new owners have re-invigorated with new layout and bar, better than normal pub-grub and improved service. The views across the Helford are worth the slippery descent from the car park. The Inn has a holiday atmosphere about it. The beach is popular with children and muck-a-bouters in boats. 01326 250625 (105/K3) ferryboatcornwall.co.uk

Halsetown Inn, Nr St Ives. This is very much a dining pub proud of its culinary heritage. With chefs trained in London and France, the food is unpretentious value-for-money and wholesome. The ambience is friendly and your charming hostess is keen to serve you fresh pints of ale whether you eat in or not. Sunday lunches are accomplished. 01736 795583 (107/J2) halsetowninn.co.uk

Pandora, Restronguet Hill. The setting has been described as magical and the thatch build a delight. It has all the ingredients for a splendid repast and a quiet drink, either overlooking the calming waters of Restronguet Creek, or inside on a settle beside a log fire. Life doesn't get much better than this. Opens at 10.30 am. 01326 372678 (102/A7) pandorainn.com

Rising Sun Inn, Altarnun. Andy Mason has cooked in Michelin Star restaurants and all over the World and brings his enthusiasm and professionalism to this popular C16 pub on the edge of Bodmin Moor. A full range of ales is on hand. The décor is minimalist with Delabole slate, flagstone floors. Camping for tents and caravans. All well suited for cyclists, horse riders and walkers. 01566 86636 (85/K3) therisingsuninn.co.uk

Rod and Line, Tideford. If you yearn for a small, traditional pub untainted by contemporary trends but with the ambience of times gone by and wish to sup from local fayre; crab, king prawns and scallops and listen to musicians as varied as the late John Martyn or Chris Jagger, none better. 01752851323 (86/D5)

Roseland Inn, Philleigh-In-Roseland. This is a friendly and often crowded pub with log fires and low ceilings. A meeting point for friends from Falmouth, Truro and St Austell and for pre-Wedding nerve, drinks – the church is close by. Pretty garden. Daily specials. Booking advised. Dogs and children welcome. Brewery. 01872 580254 (102/D6) roselandinn.co.uk

St Kew Inn. A village must have two essentials - a beautiful, historic church, and a cosy relaxed pub within spitting distance of the former. St Kew proudly boasts both. It lies hidden away down narrow lanes, far away from the hurly-burly of Rock and the Camel Estuary. The large garden is a popular lunchtime haunt. Specials board. 01208 841259 (93/K8) stkewinn.co.uk

Pint of Prawns, Cornish Arms ss

Star & Garter, 53 Old High Street, Falmouth. This restored old pub (c. 1892) has created quite a stir amongst local foodies. With a self-styled butchery on-hand to produce Family Banqueting (large joints of meat) parties, who enthuse at the cuisine and the harbour views. Happy Hour Cocktails 4-7pm. Opens from 10 for coffee and cakes. Three apartments to rent with Estuary Views. 01326 316663 (99/M9) starandgarterfalmouth.co.uk

You May Also Like to Consider:

Tinner's Arms, Zennor. This ancient and friendly pub brews its own ale, Tinners Ales, and serves quality nosh. The simple décor of settles and benches and bonhomie makes it a delight just to sit here and enjoy the scene. Dogs and children welcomed. B&B. (107/G2) tinnersarms.com

Tolcarne Inn, Newlyn. Ben Tunnicliffe has taken over this old fisherman's pub and is slowly building a name for himself (again). For Ben is a master chef and a true exponent of Cornwall's rich and varied produce. The fish comes delivered, in person, by a footman from Newlyn's Market, a mere hundred yards distant and the veg and meat are all locally produced. Brunch and coffee are served and the coastal footpath passes the front door. Dog friendly. Live Jazz on Sundays 1-3pm. 01736 363074 (107/G7) tolcarneinn.co.uk

Trengilly Wartha Inn, Constantine. This busy pub lies hidden in a valley close to the Helford River. It has a bar, bistro, function room and stunning garden with bedrooms and safari tents for hire. Dog and cricketer, friendly. 01326 340332 (105/H2) trengilly.co.uk

EAT

New Yard Restaurant ss

New Yard Restaurant, Trelowarren. Dine within an enchanting C14 estate that offers walks and trees, galore. Simple lunches, more adventurous dinners. One of Cornwall's finest eating out experiences. Open daily M-Th from 10.30, F & W/ Es at 8.30 for breakfast. 01326 221595 (105/H4) newyardrestaurant.co.uk

No 6 Restaurant & Rooms, Padstow. Paul Ainsworth's smart, chic dining establishment no doubt taking advantage of the Stein-Effect. Private dining rooms available for parties etc. 01841 532093 (92/E8) number6inpadstow.co.uk

Porthminster Beach Café, St Ives. This blend of café and serious restaurant overlooking magical white sands has struck a chord with many foodie aficionados who consider it their First Choice diner in the South West. Child friendly. Open all year from 10 for morning coffee, lunch and dinner. Barbecue Bar for burgers and snacks, next door. 01736 795353 (107/K1) porthminstercafe.co.uk

Prawn On The Lawn, 11 Duke Street, Padstow. A fishmonger and seafood bar, in one, and what a brilliant combination breaks up Mr Stein's monopoly on seafood sales. Open Tu-Sa 10-10. 01841 532223 (92/E8) prawnonthelawn.com

Restaurant Nathan Outlaw, 6 New Road, Port Isaac. In a grand position overlooking the sea and car park at top of town. A La Carte menu, yet specialises in local fish and meat dishes. His, simpler, Fish Kitchen is down in the Harbour. 01208 880896 (93/J56) nathan-outlaw.com

The Cove, Maenporth Beach, Falmouth. Arty Williams, is out to impress you with his elaborate dishes. Some would say too complex that may hide the natural ingredients best left alone for your palette? The wines are impressive and the service can be good, too. Open daily from 11. Close M in winter. 01326 251136 (105/L2) thecovemaenporth.co.uk

Oysters at No 6 ss

The Wheelhouse ss

Trewithen Restaurant, 3 Fore Street, Lostwithiel. An intimate eatery that has built a fine reputation. Roast peppers glazed with Cornish Brie or King Scallops drizzled with black pudding, and that's just for starters. Open Tu-F for lunch from 11.30am. Dinner from 6.30pm. 01208 872373 (100/D5) trewithenrestaurant.com

The Seafood Restaurant, Padstow. Needs no introduction. Rick Stein's restaurant has established a reputation since opening 40-years ago. The fish comes, literally, straight off the boats in the harbour (via a judicious by-your-leave in the Kitchen) and onto your plate. Essential to book unless you have the self-confidence of my late Father who refused to book - he was rarely turned away. 01841 532700 (92/E8) rickstein.com

The Shore, 13-14 Alverton Street, Penzance. Bruce Rennie just loves to cook (for you), especially fish and it's the Cornish shore that inspires him. He is also a passionate gardener of vegetables. Visit him and you won't be disappointed for this is one of Cornwall's finest. 01736 363444 (107/H6) theshorerestaurant.uk

You May Also Like to Consider:

The Wheelhouse Crab & Oyster Bar, Upton Slip, Falmouth. You need to book well in advance to bag a table. The service is funny, friendly, eccentric and the food; crustacea in all its arthropodic forms is to be eaten with relish and gusto. Recommend you take along a large bib/napkin. Open W-Sa 6-10. Cash only. 01326 318050 (99/M9)

The Shore, Penzance ss Nick Hook

Chapel House, Penzance ss

Chapel House, Chapel Street, Penzance. A tastefully converted intimate boutique hotel that marries Georgian architecture with contemporary furnishings. The 6-sizeable bedrooms have state-of-the-art bathrooms within them suitable for the young and body-beautiful. Since it opened it has been met with lavish praise from many a travelling hack who are most probably free and single without the encumbrance of children. Like The Scarlet (Mawgan Porth) it is marketed towards couples. 01736 362024 (107/H6) chapelhousepz.co.uk

Driftwood Hotel, Portscatho. If you find yourself by chance washed up here on the shore then you are in luck. It is, as described, decorated in pieces of driftwood. This washes over you to create a laidback ambience where you can look out over the sea, enjoy the garden and hospitality. Perhaps, find the path to the private beach. The food is quite exceptional. Bedrooms contemporarily furnished and light. No dogs. 01872 580644 (102/D8) driftwoodhotel.co.uk

Gurnard's Head Hotel. A welcome refuge if you've battled against a sou'westerly head wind on the coast path. Rich, wholesome fayre will appease a mighty appetite. Classy, arty and laidback and comfy bedrooms. One of the very best. 01736 796928 (106/F2) gurnardshead.co.uk

Hotel Endsleigh, Tamar Valley. A former fishing lodge that overlooks beautiful, ornamental gardens, a Dairy Dell, an arboretum and the Tamar Valley. The staff are friendly and discreet and its the ideal, practical stop-over after a long journey before you enter Cornwall. Two rods for hire in season for guests. Little sister to the Hotel Tresanton. 01822 870000 (83/G6) hotelendsleigh.com

Hotel Tresanton, St Mawes. This is a chic, family-friendly hotel that has raised the bar by which all are judged in Cornwall and elsewhere. It is owned by the interior designer, Olga Polizzi (Forte) and her husband the political commentator William Shawcross. Ms Polizzi has understated good taste in bucketfuls. She manages to marry comfort with contemporary art and antiques. She pulls it off, spectacularly. Nothing is too cluttered and you know that the objects: sculptures, artworks, furniture have been sort for, visualised, and positioned in situ, well in advance of your visit. Seafood is a speciality, surprise,surprise. 01326 270055 (102/B9) tresanton.com

Steak, Old Coastguards, Mousehole ss

The Idle Rocks, St Mawes.
This is a beautiful and chic hotel,
to relax, be seen and to look out
across a blue sea mirrored by
the clever and sensitive interior
designs and artworks created
for your aesthetic sustenance.
Open to non-residents. A worthy
destination for an al fresco lunch
on the Terrace. 01326 270270
(102/B9) idlerocks.com

**Kota, Harbourside,
Porthleven.** This is a restaurant
with rooms with a Polynesian
(Maori) twist. Fish is the speciality
in all its delicate and delicious
forms. Dinner is from 6-9 pm.
The bedrooms are simple and
comfortable. 01326 562407
(104/C3) kotarestaurant.co.uk

**Old Coastguard Hotel,
Mousehole.** The panoramic sea
views from the light and airy bar/
eating area may well seduce you to
stay, awhile and to sup fine ales and
wine. The food is wholesome. The
ambience, most pleasing, digestible
and inviting. 01736 731222 (106/
G8) oldcoastguardhotel.co.uk

**Portgaverne Hotel, Nr Port
Isaac.** This is a formidable
hostelry that offers delicious
food (fish of extreme freshness),
boutique-style comfort and a great
ambience in a superb location
overlooking a quaint beach. Now
with a café a stone's throw from
their front door - all with a fab
view of the little beach. Of late,
have received glowing reviews
and a deserved reputation for
interesting cuisine. 01208 880244
(93/J5) portgavernehotel.co.uk

Rick Stein's, Padstow. If
you wish to guarantee a table at
Mr Stein's formidable hostelry
then try one of these. They have
40 plush bedrooms scattered
around Padstow; in the Seafood
Restaurant, St Petroc's Hotel, St

Edmunds House, Rick Stein's
Café, Bryn Cottage and Prospect
House. All have crisp linen, superb
bathrooms and indulgent beds.
The ultimate Restaurant With
Rooms experience. 01841 532700
(92/E8) rickstein.com

St Tudy Inn, Bodmin. Emily
Scott the Proprietor is causing
quite a stir in North Cornwall.
The chattering classes are rushing
to this new hostelry to sample her
seasonal dishes, relax beside a
warm fire and to sleep the dreams
of optimists. 01208 850656
(93/M8) sttudyinn.com

You May Also Like to
Consider:

**The Old Quay House Hotel,
Fowey.** If you, like me, consider
estuaries to be chilled, calming;
the ebb and flow of the tide,
boats at anchor, whistling
halyards, bliss… continual
interest, and when the views are
stunning, you have a match made
in…? The rooms are bright and
pleasing and the al fresco dining
is a delight. 01726 833302 (100/
E8) theoldquayhouse.com

The Scarlet, Mawgan Porth.
Eco, green, sustainable living…
pure hedonism. This is what
separates this multi-million pound
investment from its peers. Is there
a paradox? It is an expensive place
to play and relax….a wish that
their example may translate into
cheaper, more plentiful options. No
children. 01637 861800 (94/C2)
scarlethotel.co.uk

The Idle Rocks ss

FAMILY & SPA HOTELS

Bedruthan Steps Hotel.
One of Cornwall's great family hotels set high on the cliff's edge overlooking Mawgan Porth beach. Awarded a Green Tourism Gold Award. It uses solar panels and light sensors, helps clean the local beach and uses local suppliers. 01637 860555 (94/C2) bedruthan.com

Budock Vean, Helford.
The Hotel On The (Helford) River is the traditional health spa to ease the pain of modern life, together with a 9 & 18 hole golf course, all set in a magical landscape where you can enjoy the 32-acre garden and its 350,000+ plants. Open for lunch/afternoon teas to non-residents. 01326 252100 (105/K2) budockvean.co.uk

Carbis Bay Hotel & Spa.
They describe themselves as the "Hotel On The Beach." Its a mix of family, corporate and wedding venue with its own pool if you don't fancy saltwater and have forgotten your wetsuit. A favourite of one Mrs Thatcher. Self-catering cottages and apartments. 01736 795311 (107/K2) carbisbayhotel.co.uk

Fowey Hall Hotel, Fowey.
This is what has been described as a luxurious family hotel. You will see lots of children making lots of noise but rarely with their parents because the nannies are in tow. The Father's are hidden in corners stuck to their smartphones. This is an expensive nursery. Kids paintings adorn the walls. Dogs and Grandmothers are allowed to venture here, too. It is exclusive and not cheap. You may ask; Are the parents allowed to dine alone? 01726 833866 (100/E8) foweyhallhotel.co.uk

Headland Hotel, Fistral Beach, Newquay.
Majestic, Awesome, Imposing ... describes this family owned and run hotel since 1989. Built in 1900 to be the South-West's finest. It overlooks Cornwall's premier surf break and if you can afford it nowhere better to hang out and learn this obsessive sport. 01637 872211 (94/A5) headlandhotel.co.uk

St Enodoc Hotel, Rock.
This is a family-friendly hotel noted for its great location, cuisine, gym and spa. It is especially devoted to families of all ages and the new

Aerial View, Budock Vean Hotel ss

Watergate Bay Hotel ss

décor is bright, comfy, colourful, and very seasidie. Special Breaks. 01208 863394 (92/E8) enodoc-hotel.co.uk

St Michael's, Falmouth. Their new spa centre with hydrotherapy pool, 60 treatments and the Special Cornish Sea Salt Room are getting local tongues wagging. A major renovation with new bedrooms and two eating areas, all overlooking Gylly Beach where you can coasteer, paddleboard and kayak. 01326 312707 (102/A10) stmichaelshotel.co.uk

St Moritz, Trebetherick. This is a quite recent development; hotel, apartments and a spa complex providing all manner of amenities that one (if you visit such places of hedonism) would expect from such a venture: gym, indoor pool, saunas etc., bar, games room and more. T 01208 862242 (92/E7) stmoritzhotel.co.uk

The Nare, Roseland Peninsula. A privately-owned hotel in the English Country House style overlooking a secluded sandy beach. Perhaps a little old-fashioned for some but such retreats are still gravely sort for in this digital age. Their values of traditional service and caring staff will delight those seeking a quintessential English style. Children and dogs (charged) are made welcome. Spa facilities. 01872 501111 (102/E7) narehotel.co.uk

Watergate Bay Hotel. A family-style, boutique hotel overlooking the stunning two-mile sandy beach. An ideal destination for a contemporary beach holiday. The hotel has three restaurants - The Beach Hut, Zacry's Restaurant and The Living Space, a Swim Club which includes an ocean view swimming pool and treatment rooms. Kids' Zone and Extreme Academy surf school. 01637 860543 (94/C3) watergatebay.co.uk

St Moritz Hotel ss

BED & BREAKFAST

Coombeshead Farm ss

Althea House, 64 Church Street, Padstow. Set in the oldest part of town opposite the Church this B&B has all the latest mod cons and comfy bedrooms. No children or pets. 01841 532579 (92/E8) altheahouse-padstow.co.uk

Coombeshead Farm, Nr Launceston. Bed and Breakfast with a difference set within 65-glorious acres of pastoral bliss. Chefs Tom and April showcase their culinary and hospitality skills by inviting you into their kitchen as they cook you your evening meal. 01566 782009 (82/B5) coombesheadfarm.co.uk

Coswarth House, 12 Dennis Road, Padstow. Escape the hustle and bustle of Padstow to this historic house affording breathtaking views across the Camel Estuary. This luxurious and B&B provides charm, style and delicious breakfasts. 07907 626084 (92/E8) coswarthhouse.com

Ednovean Farm, Perranuthnoe. This is what the experts call luxurious. Three gorgeous bedrooms decorated in designer fabrics with fab bathrooms. Surrounded by an exquisite Italian garden. 01736 711883 (107/L6) ednovean.co.uk

11 Sea View Terrace, St Ives. Neat, luxurious and immaculately turned out little B&B. Your host has a passion for art. The walls are festooned with bright, colourful paintings only matched by the fabulous view you get of St Ives from here. Self-catering apartment nearby. 01736 798440 (106/K1) 11stives.co.uk

Gardens Cottage, Prideaux. Sometimes you come across a B&B that feels just right and you don't want to leave. Hidden away in the Luxulyan Valley is Kath and Ivan Walker's exceptional and charming cottage with all the creature comforts you will ever need and much more. 01726 817195 (110/B6) gardenscottage.co.uk

Hay Barton, Tregony. Just the perfect accommodation for groups of four. The house is split into two, so the B&B area of two (light and airy) bedrooms is separate from the main house. All the fabrics are Cath Kidston and Colefax & Fowler, the beds are zip-link doubles, the breakfasts of yoghurt, grenola and farm eggs are made on the premises. Tennis Court. 01872 530288 (102/F4) haybarton.com

Ednovean B & B

Penthouse, Highcliffe Guest House

Highcliffe Guest House, 22 Melvill Road, Falmouth. This is a luxurious, family-run B&B in a smart, contemporary-furnished Edwardian villa. Perhaps, more like an intimate hotel. 01326 314466 (99/M9)
highcliffefalmouth.com

The Old Parsonage, Forrabury, Boscastle. An elegant Georgian property providing 5-star quality B&B with spacious bedrooms of great style and comfort. 01840 250339 (90/B9) old-parsonage.com

Trewornan Manor, Near Wadebridge. This is a class act. An award-winning B&B set in 25-acres with 8-acres of mature gardens. A stylish house with high ceilings, light and airy bedrooms adjoined by luxurious bathrooms. Comfortable sitting rooms and special breakfasts, and most important, gracious hosts. 01208 812359 (93/H9) trewornanmanor.co.uk

You May Also Like to Consider:

The Old Vicarage, Morwenstow. To gauge the RS Hawker Experience you must stay here in his former home. Your hosts are a mine of information. Comfortable B&B with platefuls of home cooking. Carrow's Stable to let. 01288 331369 (88/C7) rshawker.co.uk

Trevose Harbour House, 22 The Warren, St Ives. A boutique guest house with 6-lovingly designed rooms in shades of blue. Wifi, Hypnos beds and much more for your every comfort. Champagne cream teas available to assuage the stress of a Cornish sojourn, or perhaps a massage can be organized to go hand-in-hand with the Pinot Noir grape? A real find with a stones throw of Porthminster Beach and St Ives' finest Eatery. 01736 793267 (106/K1) trevosehouse.co.uk

Trewornan Manor ss

Atlantic Surf Pods ss

Atlantic Surf Pods, Nr Bude.
These eco-pods may remind
you of a Hobbits village. Each is
spacious with underground heating
within landscaped lawns. Bedding/
linen provided. Bathroom. 01288
355288 (91/H2)
atlanticsurfpods.co.uk

Barefoot Glamping, Cury.
Hobie and Woody are spacious
safari tents with two-bedrooms,
wood-fired stove, hot shower/wet
room and access to fab beaches.
Dog friendly with 12-acres of
meadows to roam. Its all in the
detail, darling! 01326 241456
(104/E5) barefoot-glamping.co.uk

**Cornish Tippi Holidays,
Tregeare.** Something different.
Hire a traditional North American
tent amidst a haven of birdsong,
wild flowers, buzzards and rabbits.
Trout fishing. No cars on site.
Warden on hand. 01208 880781
(93/L6)

**Finley & Poppy Airstreams,
Homeland Farm, Mithian.**
Children love them, Honeymooners
love them. They are a blast from
the past, and add the luxuries
on-board and the location. They
are fun. 01872 555890 (99/J1)
cornwallairstreams.co.uk

Geo Ekopod, St Clether. For
those with a spatial or mathematical
awareness these geometric
structures will seduce your inner

Einstein. All within wildflower
meadows with views of woodland
and Bodmin Moor. 01566 880248
(85/K2) ekopod.co.uk

**Henry's Campsite, The
Lizard.** If you wanted to
introduce your kids (or your
partner) to camping then start
here. Close to the village and
coastal path. The situ is rural and
the camping is your max 4-berth
tent. Everything else is exotic
from the plants to the Easter
Island décor to the poultry to the
elemental weather. 01326 290596
(105/G10) henryscampsite.co.uk

**Jack Sparrow/Tree House,
Nr St Keverne.** Designed for
a couple sharing each one and
part of a complex that includes
2 gypsy caravans and 2 cottage
lets in a remote and pastoral
landscape. 01326 281253 (105/L5)
outlandishholidays.co.uk

**Kudhva (Hideout), Nr
Trebarwith Strand.** This is
a groundbreaking eco-camp
set in 45-acres. There are 4
two-Man Kudhvas set on stilts
and 2 four-Man Kudhvas at a
lower level. Technical tree tents
in ever-changing positions. Wild
swimming, waterfalls, camp
fires and long grass to sunbathe
in. Its all about adventure and
integrating with nature or it could
be described as living in the raw.

Basically be prepared to rough it. Go for it….it will be a blast! 07917 735244 (84/C1) kudhva.com

Luxury Cornish Yurts, Little Fursdon Farm. Inspired by a visit to an African game reserve, David and Lindsey have developed three large, luxurious yurts for your every convenience and comfort. 01579 343896 (82/A10) luxurycornishyurts.co.uk

Rambling Rose Gypsy Caravan, Delancey House, Lostwithiel. This is an authentic 'Bow Top' van where you can escape the stress of modern life and discover the Romany lifestyle. Double and single beds plus space for tents. 01208 872434 (100/D4) ramblingrosecaravan.co.uk

You May Also Like to Consider:

Ruthern Valley Holidays. Nestling in a wooded valley this site offers traditional facilities for tents and caravans but also log cabins, wigwams, camping huts and bungalows. (95/L3) ruthernvalley.com

7th Rise, Philleigh. Swap your soft, digital life for new adventures: bushcraft, fishing, foraging, butchery, canoeing, archery and wild swimming. Stay in a tree house, relax in the sundowners bar, eat wild rabbit and mushrooms. Find your inner caveman or cavewoman. 07988 168457 (102/C6) 7thrise.co.uk

South Penquite Farm. If you fancy a superb view from your own canvas shelter or from inside a Mongolian Yurt, try camping in this 200-acre working farm high on Bodmin Moor and close to the fine village of Blisland. 01208 850491 (84/E7) southpenquite.co.uk

The Lambing Hut & The Hideaway Hut, Treworgey Farm, Duloe. Two shepherd's huts in secluded locations with views of the Looe Valley. Ideal for two. Private bathroom hut. It's all eco, solar and romantic. 07825 091470 (101/L6) hideawayhuts.co.uk

Trecombe Lakes, Mawnan Smith. Nanny got here first to make your stay warm and cosy. Everything you need has been thought of. Each pod has a kitchen, fridge, freezer, shower room, sink, toilets. All bed linen and towels are provided. BBQ, fire-pit and indoor heater all within stunning woodland. 01326 211850 (105/K1) trecombe-lakes.co.uk

Treen Farm, St Levan. This is first come, first served from 8.00 am. It is tranquil and open to the full force of the elements. Great when the weather is calm. Ideal for climbers, walkers, naturists and dog lovers. 07598 469322 (106/D10) treenfarmcampsite.co.uk

Lambing Hut, Treworgey Farm ss

SELF-CATERING

Caerhays Estate Luxury Holiday Cottages. From The Vean to the Fish Sheds and Lime Kilns overlooking Portholland's beach to the Old Village Hall. 0800 032 6229 (103/J5) nicheretreats.co.uk

The Vean, Caerhays. This Georgian rectory on the Caerhays Estate has been transformed into a sumptuously decorated country house (for house parties) with all things Cornish thus helping reduce their carbon footprint. B&B. Dinner. 01872 501310 (103/H5) thevean.co.uk

Ennys, St Hilary. Do you wish to get away from it all? Seek a change of scene? Then, perhaps one of the three cottages or luxurious suites will suit you. On hand, a heated pool, grass tennis court - all within 20-acres to roam and get lost. 01736 740262 (107/M5) ennys.co.uk

Halzephron House - The Cabin, The Observatory & The Cottage, Gunwalloe. The Cabin, for two romantics overlooks the coast path. The Observatory, for two nature lovers overlooks a garden of wild flowers and Mounts Bay. The rustic Cottage witnesses sunsets of unbelievable beauty, is spacious and sleeps 4. 07899 925816 (104/D5) halzephronhouse.co.uk

Higher Lank Farm, Wenfordbridge. This is unique. No question about it. A working farm specialising in the needs of parents and pre-school children (toddlers). Self-catering and guest house accommodation available. 01208 850716 (84/D6) higherlankfarm.co.uk

Kestle Barton, Manaccan. This is a community-based arts centre with ever-changing exhibitions; painting, sculpture, ceramics, and events all set within an ancient Cornish farmstead. Fabulous garden. Circular walk to Helford. Open late Mar to early Nov Tu-Sa 10.30-5. Three ancient barns have been sensitively converted into eco-green holiday lets. 01326 2318111 (105/J3) kestlebarton.co.uk

Lamorna Cove Hotel. In an exceptional location overlooking the Lamorna Valley and Cove. There are 15-luxury self-catering apartments with use of the restaurant providing fab views (open to the public), swimming pool and sauna. Child friendly. 01736 732866 (106/F9) thelamornacovehotel.com

Mesmear, St Minver. Three chic, boutique-style barns are available to rent for holidays and short breaks. Ideal for parties of up to 10, 4 and 4. Swimming pool. Private cook. 01208 869731 (93/G6) mesmear.co.uk

Wild Escapes, Tregothnan Estate ss

The Observatory, Halzephron House ss

Padstow Townhouse, 16-18 High Street. Six lavish over the top luxurious suites to slumber in and assuage your guilty hedonism. There's a pantry to feast on if you prefer to lie in *con amore*. Failing that you can book into Paul Ainsworth's No. 6 restaurant or party down at Rojano's for pizza and pasta. 01841 550950 (92/E8) paul-ainsworth.co.uk/padstow-townhouse

Porth-En-Alls, Prussia Cove. A veritable collection of historic houses and coastal cottages to hire within reach of the coast path and beach. Camping and Bakery. 01736 762014 (107/M7) prussiacove.co.uk

You May Also Like to Consider:

Shamrock Cabin, Whitsand Bay. Kick off your shoes and play at being shipwrecked in this perfectly formed log cabin atop the cliffs at Whitsand Bay. Nothing ahead of you but an endless sea view. All you need is in the cabin, and the Clifftop Café and View Restaurant, all within walking distance. Leave the car keys in the suitcase and let your cares drift away. Sleeps 2. (87/G9) shamrockcabin.co.uk

The Abbey, Abbey Street, Penzance. A sweet gem dating from the C17 lies hidden behind a walled garden and courtyard. Luxurious with fabulous fabrics, awash with colour. Call it shabby chic or an antique emporium, it oozes style, panache and will leave you with sweet memories. Now available to rent as one large domain (luxury holiday cottage) suitable for 6-12 guests. 01244 356666 (107/H6) theabbeyonline.co.uk

Trelowarren, The Lizard. Home of the Vyvyan family since 1427 and the estate that inspired Daphn Du Maurier's novel *Frenchman's Creek*. 1,000 acres of woodland and farmland surround the house for you to explore. Walled Garden Spa and sustainable buildings including 25 self-catering cottages. 01326 221224 (105/G4) trelowarren.com

Wild Escapes, Tregothnan Estate. You have a choice; from a Shepherd's Hut beside an idyllic creek to cottages in remote spots on the Lizard Peninsula. The Estate produces its own blended tea, charcoal and trees/shrubs for gardens and nurseries. (1012/C5) tregothnan.co.uk

Bodmin Moor from Hurlers Stone Circle

Chysauster Ancient Village, Nr Penzance. The best preserved Iron Age village in Cornwall. Eight circular houses with decent sized rooms. The current town planners could learn something from this site. Occupied during Roman Conquest. Access via half-mile path from road. Small reception & shop. Dogs welcome. Open daily Apr-Sept 10-6. 07831 757934 (107/H4) english-heritage.org.uk

Merry Maidens Stone Circle

Glasney College, the Collegiate Church, Penryn. Founded in 1275 by Bishop Bronescombe (of Exeter) to be the leading ecclesiastical powerhouse in medieval Cornwall. It controlled over 16 parishes, and was the setting for miracle plays in Cornish but was looted and destroyed during the Dissolution of the Monasteries, 1536-1545. The scholarship upheld here promoted the Cornish language which then languished, thereafter, and it was the Prayer Book Rebellion of 1549 that was the final nail in the coffin. Just a wall and field remain. (99/L9)

Hurlers Stone Circle, Minions. Three stone circles 110ft, 135ft and 105ft in diameter. According to legend - Men turned to stone for playing the old Cornish game of Hurling on a Sunday. It is a similar game to Australian Rules. Access is via a 1/4 mile path from road. (85/M9)

Lanyon Quoit (NT), Nr Madron. A Stone Age dolmen with 3-uprights and a Capstone re-erected c.1824. (106/F4)

Men-An-Tol, Nr Morvah. A large circular slab with a hole pierced through the centre is set between 2-upright slabs. Famous for its legendary magical healing

Trevethy Quoit, Bodmin Moor

powers - children were passed through to cure them of rickets (and insolence). (106/E4)

Merry Maidens Stone Circle, Nr Lamorna. These 19-stones form the perfect circle. Legend has it – of girls turned to stone for dancing on a Sunday. (106/F9)

Plain-An-Gwarry, St Just-In-Penwith. Circular embankment (cattle pen) where old Cornish miracle plays were performed. (106/B6)

The Cheesewring, Nr Minions. An extraordinary formation of granite slabs weathered by wind and rain. A Bronze Age cup (now residing in the British Museum) was found in a grave on Stowe's Hill. (85/M8)

Trethevy Quoit, Tremar. An impressive Neolithic dolmen. The 6-uprights support a massive Capstone, pierced by a circular hole. (85/M10)

Zennor Quoit. One of England's largest dolmens. A double-chambered tomb with a massive slab. Pieces of Neolithic pottery discovered here. Park in lay-by (St Ives road) below the Eagle's Nest (the late Patrick Heron's home). A good 40-minute ascent through thistles and bracken. Head towards Zennor Heights and bear left opposite The Carne, a shack (legend has it that the Occultist Aleister Crowley lived here) and the Dolmen will appear in ten minutes on your right. (107/G2)

Lanyon Quoit

GREAT CHURCHES

Launcells Church

Altarnun, St Nonna.
Superb C16 church. The tall
perpendicular tower rises to 109
ft. Norman font. C16 bench ends.
Known locally as 'The Cathedral
of the Moors'. Overlooks an
attractive linear village. (85/K4)

**Blisland, St Protus & St
Hyacinth.** Wonderfully restored
church in village with attractive
village green. C15 granite tower
and Norman font. C15 brasses.
(84/D8)

Bodmin, St Petroc. In the C6
Cornwall's patron saint, St Petroc
founded a priory here. Later in the
C9 a monastery was established
and in the Middle Ages the town
became an important religious
centre. The present church was
mainly built in the C15. Norman
font, Monuments and Wagon roof.
(100/C1)

Launcells, St Swithins.
Fortunate to be the only Cornish
church not tampered with by the
Victorians. Wall painting and
60 carved bench ends. Fabulous
wagon roofs, note the carvings. All
is situated in a divine valley. (91/J2)

**Launceston, St Mary
Magdalene.** Noted for the
famous exterior carved granite
panels of foliage and shields that
cover most of the walls. C14 tower,
and a rare painted pulpit. (82/D2)

**Morwenstow, St John the
Baptist.** Famous for the C19
poet-vicar, R S Hawker who
buried many shipwrecked sailors
in his churchyard. Impressive
Norman doorway, wagon roof and
wall paintings. In superb location
overlooking the Atlantic Ocean.
(88/B7)

St Germanus, St Germans.
Founded as an Augustinian Priory,
and later, a Cathedral in the Anglo-
Saxon period. Only the South Aisle
and Nave remain. Magnificent
Norman doorway, and East Window
glass by the pre-Raphaelite, Edward
Burne-Jones. (86/E6)

St Neot. Imposing building in
scenic valley famous for the 15
medieval stained glass windows.
Perhaps, the finest glass in the West
Country. (101/H1)

Tintagel, St Materiana. Of
Norman origin and Catholic
empathy, this church defies
erosive nature and the storms she
encounters in its isolated clifftop
position. Visit on a dark, moody
day and be impressed. (92/L2)

Truro Cathedral. The first
English Cathedral to be built since
St Paul's. An imposing building
designed by John Pearson, in the
Gothic style, 1880-1910. With three
soaring spires, and an unrivalled
collection of stained glass. Refectory
for light meals, 10-4. Open M-Sa
7.30-6, Su 9-7. Shop and Chapter
House from 10. (102/B4)

Adam & Eve Window, St Neots

The Roof & Nave, Truro Cathedral

Restormel Castle, Lostwithiel ss

Caerhays Castle & Gardens.
60 acres of informal woodland
gardens created by J C Williams
who had sponsored plant hunting
expeditions to China. Noted
for camellias, magnolias and
rhododendrons. Spring Garden
open daily mid-Feb to mid-June,
10-5. Castle Tours (booking
advised) from mid-March to mid-
June, 11.30, 1.00 & 2.30pm.
(103/J3) caerhays.co.uk

**Castle An Dinas, Nr Indian
Queens.** Four massive concentric
rings; crowned by 'Roger's Tower',
an C18 folly. Iron Age pottery
found. (95/H5)

**Fowey, St Catherine's Castle
(EH).** Few remains survive of this
former blockhouse built in 1536
to house a protective chain across
the harbour mouth in accord
with Henry VIII's military policy.
Viewpoint. (100/E9)

Launceston Castle (EH).
Norman castle built in c.1070
with timber. It was the main seat
of Robert de Mortain brother of
William the Conqueror. Rebuilt
C12-13. Good example of a
"motte and bailey" structure.
Open daily Apr-Sept 10-6. (82/
D2) english-heritage.org.uk

**Pendennis Castle (EH),
Falmouth.** Built 1544-46 in the
age of cannon and gunpowder as
one of a chain of castles Henry
VIII erected from 1538 to deter
French Invasion. Circular Keep
with drawbridge, portcullis, spy
holes and spiral staircase. Superb
viewpoint. To the south east the
blockhouse built on the rocks.
Open daily Apr-Sept 10-6.
(102/A10) english-heritage.org.uk

Pengersick Castle. Fortified
Tudor manor c. 1500 with
evidence of an Apothocarian
garden in the C14 to be renovated.
"The most haunted house in the
UK". With the death of the last
owner, the late Angela Evans, the
trustees have set forth to restore
the castle with a grand opening
planned. (104/A2) pengersickcastle.
com

**Restormel Castle (EH),
Lostwithiel.** A model of
military architecture; classically
symmetrical with circular moat,
and strategically positioned
allowing breathtaking views across
the River Fowey. Built c.1100 with
C13 additions. Owned by Simon
de Montfort and Richard Earl of
Cornwall. Open daily Apr-June
10-5, July-Aug 10-6, Sept 10-5.
(100/D8) english-heritage.org.uk

St Mawes Castle (EH). Built
in 1540-43 as a link in Henry
VIII's chain of coastal defences. A
fortress of striking symmetry; trefoil

shaped with gun emplacements, drawbridge and heraldic decorations and all set in sub tropical gardens. Superb viewpoint. Open daily Apr-Sept 10-6. (102/B9) english-heritage.org.uk

St Michael's Mount (NT), Marazion. A legendary place of romance and pilgrimage and a child's dream of a fairy castle. Originally the site of a Benedictine chapel established by Edward the Confessor. In the C14 the spectacular castle was added. Later to be used as a nunnery and military fortress before the St Aubryn family purchased it in 1659 living here ever since. Church dates from 1275. Exquisite Blue Drawing Room with Chippendale furniture. Pictures by Gainsborough and the Cornish Artist, John Opie. Harbour, railway. Open Feb 1/2 term, then mid-Mar to 31 Oct M-F & Su 10.30-5, Guided tours late Feb to mid-Mar if weather and tides permit. Church opens on Sunday at 10.30 for 11am Service. Gardens open mid-Apr to June M-F 10.30-5, July to Sept Th & F only from 10.30. Restaurant and shop open daily Apr-Oct. Special family ticket available. Please Note: access on foot over the causeway at low tide or during summer months only by ferry at high tide (return ferry tickets

St Mawes Castle

should not be taken). Make sure the Mount is open before crossing on the ferry! (C11) Estate Office for winter openings: 01736 710265 (107/K6) stmichaelsmount.co.uk

Tintagel Castle (EH). An early Celtic settlement 350-800 AD later developed into this island fortress by the Earls of Cornwall in the C12 and C13s. Fragments of the Great Hall c.1250, the gate and walls survive. The wild and windswept coast married with the romantic legends of King Arthur and encouraged by Geoffrey of Monmouth and Tennyson's Idyll (although doubted by scholars) provide an atmosphere of mystery and wonder. New bridge has added controversy to the site. Open as locally advertised. (93/L2) english-heritage.org.uk

Pendennis Castle ss

HISTORIC BUILDINGS

Bodmin Jail. A formidable and eerie building that holds secrets to shock. Life in the C18 was cheap and public executions were rife and blood-curdling. Fine café/restaurant. A 63-bedroom boutique hotel is planned within this extraordinary build alongside a Bat Sanctuary. Open all year from 9.30. 01208 76992 (100/B1) bodminjail.org

Jamaica Inn & Museums, Bolventor. A former old coaching inn and inspiration for Daphne du Maurier's novel. Bars, restaurants, accommodation & gift shops. Attractions include the Daphne du Maurier Room, 'The Smugglers at Jamaica Inn'. Inn open daily, all year. 01566 86250 (85/H6) jamaicainn.co.uk

Lizard Lighthouse Heritage Centre. Large, famous building completed in 1752 with alterations in 1903. Stands amid treacherous coast haunted by many shipwrecks. Renovated Engine Room. Climb the lighthouse tower. Visitor Centre open mid-March to Oct M-F, weather permitting. (105/G10) trinityhouse.co.uk

Mount Edgcumbe House & Park. Sensitively restored Tudor mansion in beautiful landscaped parkland. Formal English, French and Italian Gardens. National Camellia Collection. Park and gardens open daily all year. House and Earl's Garden open Apr-Sept Sa-Th 11-4.30. 01752 822236 (87/K8) mountedgcumbe.gov.uk

Pencarrow House. Georgian house set in extensive grounds. Fine collections of pictures, furniture and porcelain. Café, gift and plant shop, and children's play area. 01208 841369. House open daily from Apr-Sept (gardens from 1 Mar-Oct 10-5) except F & Sa 11-5. (93/L10) pencarrow.co.uk

Pendeen Lighthouse. Built in 1900 to protect vessels from Wra Rocks around Pendeen Watch. The lighthouse keeper's cottages are now let as holiday cottages and the automatic fog signal is controlled via a telemetry link from the Trinity House Operational Control Centre in Harwich. (106/C3) trinityhouse.co.uk

Pencarrow House & Gardens ss

View of Port Eliot ss

Prideaux Place, Padstow.
Home of the Prideaux-Brune
family. Filled with treasures,
pictures, portraits, porcelain and
exquisite furniture. Location for
many of Rosamund Pilcher's TV
series. Open Easter week, then
mid-May to early Oct Su-Th
1.30-4. Grounds and tearoom from
10.30-5. 01841 532411 (92/E8)
prideauxplace.co.uk

The Great Hall, Prideaux Place ss

**King Arthur's Great Hall &
Hall of Chivalry, Tintagel**. A
magnificent hall built in memory
of King Arthur and his Knights,
using 50 types of Cornish stone
and 70 stained glass windows. The
Arthurian Experience tells the
story of Arthur and his Knights.
Dogs welcome. Open daily Mar-
Oct M-Sa 10-5 01840 770526
(93/M2) kingarthursgreathalls.co.uk

Trelowarren, Nr Helston.
Home of the Vyvyan family since
1427 and now a pioneering Eco-
Timeshare development. Acres of
woodland and farmland surround
the house. Cornish herbs and
woodland walks. Cornwall Crafts
Association shop. 25 self-catering
cottages. Time Share, Garden
Spa and New Yard Restaurant for
lunch and dinner. Garden open
to customers 11-5 in season (no
dogs). 01326 222105 (105/G4)
trelowarren.co.uk

Trereife Park, Penzance.
Queen Anne manor house and
home to the Le Grice family
whose descendant, Valentine Le
Grice, was a poet and friend to
the Romantics, Wordsworth and
Coleridge. Fine plasterwork and
wood panelling. The garden is
classically Cornish with parterres
and terraces. B&B. House Open as
locally advertised. 01736 362750
(107/G6) trereifepark.co.uk

Camel Valley Vineyard ss

Boscastle's Farm Shop & Café.
Home reared Devon cattle and livestock produce award-winning beef, lamb and pork. All-day breakfasts, lunches, teas in café. A mile out of the village beside the B3263. Open 9-5. 01840 250827 (90/B8) boscastlefarmshop.co.uk

Camel Valley Vineyards.
Cornwall's leading vineyard and viticulturist noted for its award-winning wines cultivated from the 8,000 vines that lie in a south-facing valley. Tasting, shop and pre-booked tours. Open M-F 10-5 (Sa East-Sept). Advised to bring your own chauffeur or cash for a taxi home to your billet. 01208 77959 (95/M2) camelvalley.com

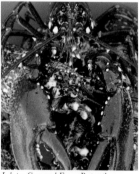

Lobster, Curgurrell Farm, Portscatho

Cornish Cyder Farm, Penhallow.
40 varieties of fruit products, from scrumpies to chutneys. Farm animals and tractor rides. Guided tour of museum, distillery and underground cellars. Restaurant. Open daily. 01872 573356 (99/L1) thecornishcyderfarm.co.uk

Curgurrell Farm, Portscatho.
The farmer is Portscatho's Harbour Master who owns a bevy of lobster and crab pots. You can drop in and buy freshly caught crustacea and fish caught off-the-line; bass, plaice etc. Open daily Apr- Oct & Dec 10-5. Self-catering let. 01872 580243 (102/E7) curgurrellfarmshop.co.uk

Great Cornish Food Store, Tregurra Park, Truro.
This is an independent grocery store with its own butchery, fishmonger and chef-led café, deli and takeaway. The store works with in excess of 200 Cornish suppliers and producers with the aim of providing quality, authentic and traceable products that are great value-for-money. The store is set within the Waitrose complex. Open daily Monday to Saturday from 8am - 7pm Sunday from 10am - 4pm & Bank Holidays 9am-5pm. 01872 306060 (102/B3) greatcornishfood.co.uk

Polgoon Vineyard ss

Nancarrow Farm Feasts, Zelah. For nine generations the same family have ploughed the earth here at Nancarrow (meaning in Cornish *Nans - valley* and *carow- stag*). A 100-acre organic farm host to weddings, corporate events, accommodation and Feast Nights. The Feast Nights are open to 130 carnivorous guests who can delight in the season's harvest. Their award-winning organic beef and lamb feature strongly in their menus. Advised to book early. 01872 487099 (99/M1) nancarrowfarm.co.uk

Padstow Farm Shop, Trethilick Farm. In need of organic beef, fresh lamb and pork sausages, cakes, ale and Cornish wines? Then, make a trip down a country lane to this emporia of delights. 01841 533060 (92/D8) padstowfarmshop.co.uk

Polgoon Vineyard, Rosehill, Penzance. You can enjoy tours and tastings and get an insight into the making of their award-winning Rosé and Sparkling wines, ciders and soft drinks. Farm shop. Open M-Sa 9-5.30, Su from Easter. 01736 333946 (107/G6) polgoon.com

Roskilly's, St Keverne. Working farm selling their farm produce; ice cream, fudge, clotted cream, preserves etc. Restaurant and tearoom. Furniture and glass gallery. Open daily 10-dusk (W/Es in winter). Footpaths through woods, meadows and ponds. Holiday cottages. 01326 280479 (105/L6) roskillys.co.uk

Trevibban Mill Vineyard & Orchards. You can take the Sunday (pre-booked) 3-hour walking tour, or just sample a dry, elegant white suffused with citrus aromas, or a punchy, lengthy, red full-bodied and balanced, accompanied by cheese or charcuterie. Open daily in summer, 12-6, winter W-Su 12-5. Another viticultural experience to succour with the helping hand of a chauffeur. 01841 541413 (94/F1) trevibbanmill.com

Roskilly's Dairy Farm, St Keverne

Antony House Copyright ©National Trust Images/Andrew Butler

Antony House & Gardens, Nr Torpoint. Built for Sir William Carew from 1711-1721 and considered the most distinguished example of early C18 architecture in Cornwall. Colonnades, panelled rooms and family portraits. Location for film "Alice In Wonderland". Open East to Oct Tu, W, Th, Su & BHMs 12-5, Garden Mar to Oct Sa-Th except M 11-5. 01752 812191 (87/H6)

Cotehele House, Nr Calstock. Medieval house of grey granite built from 1485-1627 in a romantic position overlooking the River Tamar and Devon beyond. For centuries the Edgcumbe family home containing their original furniture, C17 tapestries, armour and needlework. The gardens lie on several levels. Medieval dovecote. Ancient clock in Chapel. Refreshments and shop. Open daily except F (house closed), mid-Mar to early Nov 11-5 (4.30 in Oct). Gardens open all year 10.30-dusk. 01579 351346 (87/H1)

East Pool Mine (Cornish Mines & Engines), Nr Camborne. These two great beam engines built in 1892, were used for pumping water and winding men and ore up and down from depths of over 550 metres. Site includes the Industrial Discovery Centre at East Pool. Open daily except M & Su late Mar to Oct 10.30-5. Mitchell's Engine House open 12-4. 01209 315027 (98/E5)

Glendurgan Garden Copyright ©National Trust Images/Andrew Butler

The Great Hall, Lanhydrock ss

Glendurgan Garden, Mawnan.
A valley garden of great beauty with fine trees and shrubs; a maze, a giant's stride, a wooded valley of primulas and bluebells runs down to the Helford River. Garden open daily mid-February to end October 10.30-5.30. 01326 252020 (105/K2)

Godolphin House, Nr Helston.
Romantic Tudor and Stuart Mansion, c.1475. The Godolphin family's courtly ambitions and taste are expressed in the evolving design of the house. Tin mining provided wealth for this family of entrepreneurs, soldiers, poets and officials. C16 and C17 English furniture. Garden open daily 10-5, House open first Sa-Th of every month Feb-Oct except August. 01736 763194 (98/B10) godolphinhouse.com

Lanhydrock House, Nr Bodmin.
This is Cornwall's grandest house. C17 but largely rebuilt after the fire in 1881. Superb Victorian kitchens, magnificent plaster ceilings depicting scenes from the Old Testament and a Long Gallery 116 feet long. C17 Gatehouse. Fine shrub and formal gardens. Woodland walks. Restaurants. Shop. Open daily mid-Mar to early Nov except M when House only closed, but open BH Ms 11-5.30 (-5 in Oct), Gardens open all year 10-6. 01208 265950 (100/C3)

Levant Mine & Beam Engine, Pendeen.
The oldest steam engine in Cornwall restored after 50-years. Open mid-Mar to Oct Su-F & BHs 10.30-4. 01736 786156 (106/B4)

Tintagel, The Old Post Office.
A miniature C14 manor house used in the C19 as a post office. Open daily mid-Mar to Oct 11-4 (5 in Apr/May, 5.30 June-Sept). (93/M2)

Trelissick Garden, Nr Feock.
Extensive park, farmland and woods. A large garden lovely in all seasons with beautiful views over the Fal Estuary and Falmouth Harbour. Woodland Walks beside River Fal. Open daily from 10.30. Parkland open dawn-dusk. 01872 862090 (102/B6)

Trengwainton Garden, Nr Penzance.
Large shrub garden with a vast collection of rhododendrons. Colourful in spring and early summer. Views across Mounts Bay. Open mid-Feb to 30 Oct Su-Th 10.30-5. 01736 363148 (106/F6)

Trerice, Nr Newquay.
A delightful, small and secluded Elizabethan manor house rebuilt in 1571 containing magnificent fireplaces, plaster ceilings, oak and walnut furniture. Small lawn mower museum. Refreshments. Open daily late Feb to Oct from 10.30. 01637 875404 (94/C7)

Trewidden ss

Antony Woodland Gardens.
100-acres of sprawling woodland, 103 magnolias, 300 types of camellias and a plethora of azaleas and rhododendrons bordering the River Lynher. Open daily except M & F Mar-Oct 11- 5. 01752 812364 (87/H6) antonywoodlandgarden.com

Bosahan Garden, Manaccan.
Lieing close to the Helford River Bosagan has a micro-climate that encourages exotic palms, rhododendrons, azaleas and trees from southern climes. Open mid-Apr to early July M-F 10.30- 4.30. 01326 231351. (105/J3)

Bosvigo. A plantsman's garden best seen in summer (June-Aug); with a series of enclosed and walled gardens and their herbaceous borders. Nursery. 01872 275774. Open Mar-Sept W Th & F 11-6. 01872 275774 (102/A4) bosvigo.com

Eden Project. The world-famous project that converted old china clay pits into vast steel-framed domes housing a tropical rain forest and a Mediterranean climate. This project of great vision and ambition has drawn visitors in their hundreds of thousands since opening in Spring 2000. It has also opened the floodgates of new architecture into the county. YHA and camp site. Open daily from 10. 01726 811911 (100/B7) edenproject.com

Enys Gardens. The oldest garden in Cornwall and the home of Robert de Enys who lived here during the reign of Edward 1. Bluebells galore! Dogs on lead. Open Apr-Sept Tu & Th 2-5 and Su 11-5. 01326 259885 (99/L8) enysgardens.org.uk

Heligan Gardens. With over 200 acres to explore be sure to give yourself a full day to enjoy these stunning pleasure grounds; a Living Museum of C19 horticulture and one of the most inspiring restoration projects in history. For its success gave rise to the Eden Project. Open daily, all year from 10. 01726 845100 (103/K3) heligan.com

Penjerrick Gardens. Described as a Jungle Garden. Yet it is essentially a spring-flowering garden of 16 acres with an abundance of camellias, azaleas, rhododendrons and tree ferns. There are magnificent trees, pond gardens, bamboo and a woodland walk. 01872 870105. Open Mar-Sept W, F & Su 1.30-4.30. 01872 870105 (105/L1) penjerrickgarden.co.uk

Sculpture Garden, Tremenheere

Trebah Gardens. Magical sub-tropical ravine gardens running down to private beach on Helford River, a canvas of ever-changing colour from Spring to Autumn. A garden for the plantsman and artist, and a paradise for children. 01326 252200. Open daily, all year from 10. (105/K2) trebahgarden. co.uk

Tregrehan Gardens. Woodland garden created in the C19 by Carlyon family. Nursery. Camellias. Holiday cottages. 01726 814389. Open mid-Mar to end May, W-F, Su & BHMs 10.30-5, then W mid-June to end Aug, 1-4.30. (100/B8) tregrehan.org

Tremenheere Sculpture Gardens, Nr Gulval. This is a relatively new venture that opened in 2012 and all is set in a sheltered valley with stupendous views across the Bay. Within the woods, streams and sub-tropical plantings are sculptures. Kitchen provides the food and is in itself a worthy destination. Gardens open daily 10.30-4.30, Kitchen 10-4, Gallery Tu-Su 11-4.30. 01736 448089 (107/H5) tremenheere.co.uk

You May Also Like to Consider:

The Japanese Garden, St Mawgan. Set in a sheltered valley. Features Water, Stroll and Zen gardens. Woodland garden. Shop and plant centre. Open daily Mar-Oct 10-6. 01637 860116 (94/D3) japanesegarden.co.uk

Trewidden Garden. Originally planted by T B Bolitho in the late C19 these 15-acres provide a profusion of colour especially in Spring; bluebells, camellias, magnolias. 01736 363021 Open daily late Feb to mid-Sept 10.30-5.30. 01736 363021 (106/F7) trewiddengarden.co.uk

Trewithen Gardens. 30-acre garden renowned for its magnificent collection of camellias, rhododendrons, magnolias and many rare trees and shrubs surrounded by traditional parkland landscaped in the C18. Sculpture fountain. Gardens open daily Mar-June 2-5. House closed for renovations. 01726 883647 (102/F2) trewithengardens.co.uk

Eden Project ss

The Cheesewring , Bodmin Moor

Bodmin Moor. A wild and remote landscape of sudden mists and mysterious legend. A vegetation of boggy moorland, open heathland, granite tors and hidden valleys. The highest point is Brown Willy (1,377ft). This remote wilderness, far from the dangerous beasts of the forest and plains attracted prehistoric man. Hut circles, burial grounds and stone circles litter the landscape. An exhilarating place for pony trekking and walking but beware of sudden mists! (85/K6)

Carrick Roads. 4-mile long drowned valley fed by 5 tributaries. Boat trips from Falmouth to Truro and St Mawes from Prince of Wales, Pier. At Custom House Quay trips to Helford Passage and Roseland in summer season. Popular with Yachtsmen. (102/B9)

Combe Valley Nature Trail. This trail starts at Combe Cottages to follow a green and peaceful wooded valley rich in oakwoods, honeysuckle and birdlife - buzzards, woodpeckers, dippers. Nearby Stowe Barton home of Sir Richard Grenville, County Sheriff of Cornwall in 1577 who was immortalised in Tennyson's poem *The Revenge.* (88/C8)

Froe Creek. Haven for wildfowl and herons. Start of 6 1/2 mile walk from Porth Farm car park around peninsula to Towan Beach. Coast path to Zone Point, Carricknath Point, St Anthony and back. Shorter 3 1/2 mile walk, westwards direct to Porthmellin Head and St Anthony. (102/C10)

Fowey River. Rises on Bodmin Moor and is especially beautiful between Lostwithiel and Doublebois where it runs beside richly wooded riverbanks. Fly Fishing for brown trout and sea trout is possible. Respryn Bridge is a fine spot. If estuary life harkens you visit St Winnow. Enchanting. (100/J2)

Goonhilly Downs. The high central plateau of the Lizard Peninsula and of great interest to botanists, geologists and archaeologists. It has a profusion of wild flowers where the summer air is acute with scent. Buzzards soar up high. Green serpentine rock forms. Croft Pascoe Nature Reserve. (105/H6)

Helford River. This is a beautiful tree-lined (hollies and oaks) tidal river with romantic creeks (Frenchman's Creek) and inlets with spare, ancient trees and forgotten wrecks sunken in the mud flats. The picturesque villages of Durgan, Helford and Porth Navas and St Anthony bear witness to those 'muck abouters' in boats. (105/J3)

Kennall Vale Nature Reserve, Ponsanooth. A former gunpowder factory was located in this reserve of broadleaf woodland, waterfalls, open glades and footpaths. Easy access. (99/J7)

Loe Pool & Penrose Estate. The largest natural lake in the West Country inhabited by wildfowl and surrounded by rhododendrons and wild flowers. In evidence since the C14, the River Cober was blocked by silt and the Loe Bar developed to form a bank of flint shingle. Cycling Trails for families have been developed around the Estate. Apple Festival in the Autumn. Bridleways are being developed for horse riding. Stables Café open daily in summer, W/Es in winter. (104/D3)

St Nectan's Glen, Nr Tintagel. C5 hermitage of St Nectan. St Nectan's Kieve (60ft) Waterfall is one of Cornwall's most sacred sites and a place of beauty and tranquillity. Two additional waterfalls and a lovely woodland walk is available to discover. Cabin Café for cream teas and light meals. Open daily Apr-Oct 9.30-5.30, Nov to mid-Feb 10.30-3.30, Mid-Feb to Mar 10-4. (93/M2) st-nectansglen.co.uk

You May Also Like to Consider:

Valency Valley, Nr Boscastle. Two-hour walk up dreamlike valley through woodland to St Juliot's Church where Thomas Hardy met his first wife Emma Gifford, the vicar's sister. (90/C9)

Cycling the Penrose Estate

AK Wildlife Cruises, Falmouth ss

AK Wildlife Cruises, Falmouth Marina. Wildlife and sight-seeing tours, whale and dolphin watching, film trips, corporate hire and special occasion trips. Indeed an opportunity to see Falmouth Bay and the surrounding coastal waters by season. The boat is a "Flybridge Aquabell Sports Cruiser", - with full central heated indoor seating area and open outdoor seating, too. Hot drinks and snacks available and comfortable loo facilities. 4-hour and 7-hour (all day) trips available. 01326 316098 (102/A9) akwildlifecruises.co.uk

Cornish Birds of Prey Centre. Over 50 birds ranging from falcons, hawks and owls. Waterfowl Lake plus coarse fishing. Flights twice daily at 12 & 2.30. Open Apr-Oct Tu-Sa & all of Aug 10-5. 01637 880544 (95/G3) cornishbirdsofprey.co.uk

Falmouth - Orca Sea Safaris, Discovery Quay. Your chance to see dolphins, seals and seabirds galore. A spectacular coastal safari in an open speed boat. Quite an adrenalin rush to be had. Not for the faint hearted. 01326 214928 (102/A9) orcaseasafaris.co.uk

Monkey Sanctuary. The first protected breeding colony of Amazon Woolly Monkeys in the world. Four species of Monkeys cared for. Bat Cave & Wildlife Room. Tree Top Café for refreshments. Open W/Es Apr to Oct & 1/2 terms & Holidays W-Su. 11-4.30. 01503 262532 (86/B7) monkeysanctuary.org

National Seal Sanctuary. Rescuing, rehabilitating and releasing seal pups from around our coasts. The Sanctuary is also a permanent home for seals and sea lions unable to return to the wild. Feeding Talks throughout the day, Nature Trail Walk, Seal Hospital, Nursery, Convalescent and Resident Pools. Café/gift shop. Open daily 11-4. (105/G3) sealsanctuary.sealifetrust.org

Newquay - Blue Reef Aquarium, Towan Beach. Overlooks one of England's most popular surf beaches and houses the creatures which live beneath those crashing waves!

Monkey Sanctuary Trust, Looe ss

National Lobster Hatcher, Padstow ss

Journey through a wonderland of underwater worlds from the Cornish coastline to the undersea gardens of the Mediterranean. Café/gift shop. Open daily from 10. 01637 878134 (94/A5) bluereefaquarium.co.uk

Newquay Zoo, Trenance Gardens. 13-acres of exotic gardens; Tropical House, Village Farm, Hedgehog Hospital, Dragon maze, children's play area. Many endangered species. Picnics. Café. Open daily from 10. 01637 873342 (94/B5) newquayzoo.org.uk

Padstow – National Lobster Hatchery, South Quay. Visitor centre and research laboratories promote the conservation and management of coastal marine resources. Open daily, all year from 10. 01841 533877 (92/E9) nationallobsterhatchery.co.uk

Paradise Park, Hayle. Wildlife conservation sanctuary, with 400 birds and animals, in 100 aviaries in a 7 acre garden. Indoor play area. "Eagles of Paradise" flying displays. World Parrot Trust. Cornish Otter Sanctuary. Open daily, all year from 10. 01736 753365 (107/M3) paradisepark. org.uk

Porfell Animal Land. Designed for all ages to enjoy domestic and exotic wild animals; ocelots, wallabies, meerkats, lemurs, iguanas with play area and walks in fine countryside. Open 1/2 term, then daily Apr-Oct 10-6. 01503 220211 (101/H5) porfell.co.uk

You May Also Like to Consider:

Screech Owl Sanctuary, Goss Moor. Rescue and rehabilitation centre for sick and injured owls. Flying displays. Guided tours. Tearoom. Open daily from 10. 01726 860182 (95/G5) screechowlsanctuary.co.uk

Tamar Otter Sanctuary. Set in 20-acres of mature woodland where three species of deer roam free and where British and Asian Otters live in large semi-natural enclosures. Waterfowl lakes, nature trail and picnic area. Tearoom. Open daily Apr-Oct 10.30-6. 01566 785646 (91/L10) tamarotters.co.uk

Newquay Zoo ss

Penwith Gallery, St Ives ss

Anima Mundi, Street-an-Pol, St Ives. A leading gallery with contemporary paintings and ceramics at the leading edge, in a three-storey building. Open Mar-Oct M-Sa 10-5. (107/K1) animamundi.com

Beside The Wave, 10 Arwenack St., Falmouth. Established in 1989 to provide an outlet for Cornwall's leading contemporary artists and craftsmen. Open M-Sa 10-5, Su 11.30-4. (99/M9) beside-the-wave.co.uk

Circle Contemporary, Hawksfield A39, Wadebridge. If you are seeking works of contemporary art then a visit to this attractive bright space will enlighten your day. The proprietors wish to provide work that is visually acute, thoughtful and beautiful. Only You can judge that. Whatever, I am sure these pieces will invite conversation and opinons. Failing that you can head to Strong Adolfos for a strong coffee and some sustenance. Open M-Sa 10-4. 01208 813220 (93/F10) circlecontemporary.co.uk

Cornwall Contemporary, 1 Parade St., Penzance. A leading independent gallery run by Sara Brittain who has had a long and happy association with West Country artists. Open M-Sa 10-5. (107/H6) cornwallcontemporary.com

Jackson Foundation Gallery, North Row, St Just. Kurt Jackson paints canvasses inspired by the Cornish land and sea. The gallery also explores art and sculpture its many forms with regular exhibitions. All in this highly eco-green space. Open W-F 10-5, Sa 10-2. 01736 787638 (106/C6) jacksonfoundationgallery.com

Lander Gallery, Lemon Street Market, Truro. Spacious open gallery displays C19 and C20 Cornish Masters to contemporary fine art and crafts. Coffee shop. Open M-Sa 9-6 (102/B4) landergallery.co.uk

Circle Congtemporary ss

Neil Pinkett, Cornwall Contemporary

Lemon Street Gallery, Truro. A quality gallery whose aim is to introduce the British Art Scene to Cornwall. Modern and Contemporary art, sculpture and ceramics. Open M-Sa 10.30-5.30. (102/B4) lemonstreetgallery.co.uk

Lighthouse Gallery, 54 Causewayhead. An affordable mix of contemporary and traditional work. Much by Cornish artists. Open M-Sa from 10. 01736 350555 (107/H6) lighthouse-gallery.com

Market House Gallery, The Square, Marazion. This, the largest gallery in the village specialises in C20 Cornish artists and holds 6 exhibitions each year of both one-person and group shows. Sculpture, glass and ceramics are also displayed. Open daily. 01736 719019 (107/K6) markethousegallery.co.uk

New Gallery, 5 The Square, Portscatho. This gallery is the brainchild of Chris Insoll and has

Neil Canning, Lemon Street Gallery, Truro

been described as The Cornish Art Colony. It represents established West Country artists and is a treasure trove of unexpected pleasures. Open Th, F & Sa 10-12.30, 2-5. 01872 580445 (102/D8) chrisinsoll.com

You May Also Like to Consider:

Penwith Gallery, Back Rd West, St Ives. This is a fabulous work space and home of the Penwith Society of Arts who hold continuous exhibition of paintings, sculpture and ceramics. Open M-Sa 10-5. (107/K1) penwithgallery.com

Porthilly Gallery. Jethro Jackson's location will inspire you to paint and perhaps take home a signature of Cornwall's landscape. Open daily in season. 01208 863844 (92/F8) porthillygallery.co.uk

Tyler Gallery, 12 Brook St., Mousehole. Established by Newlyn born Essex Tyler who specialises in ornamemtal Raku pottery based on old Japanese methods. Also, paintings and jewellery. Open daily 10.30-5. 01736 731109 (107/G8) essextyler.com

Yew Tree Gallery, Morvah. Worth the journey to visit these converted stables facing the Atlantic that puts on exhibitions of Applied and Fine Art. Sculpture and organic gardens. Open Tu-Sa 10.30-5.30, Su 2-5. (106/D4) yewtreegallery.com

BUYING CRAFTSMANSHIP

Adrian Brough Pottery, Fore St., Lelant. Beautifully decorated pots of marine life, using ceramic styles from Portugal and Korea. Open M-F 9-5, W/Es by appoint. B&B. 01736 755515 (107/L3) adrianbroughpottery.co.uk

Ann Thomas, Truro. Ann is a maker of contemporary objects working with materials of sharp contrast, fine porcelain, peaty black stoneware. Forms are thrown, cut, torn and riveted touched with gold leaf and vermillion. Her work is informed by uncompromising attention to detail and craftsmanship, influenced equally by the quiet, still, Japanese aesthetic and a deep engagement with the Australian landscape. 01872 278017 (102/B4) ann-thomas.com

Falmouth Pottery, Webber Street, Falmouth. With clay from St Agnes, a glaze of feldspar (Cornish stone and ash) and French charm, you have a centre of craftsmanship and joie de vivre

(pots). Open M-Sa 11-5. 01326 211663 (99/M9) michelfrancois.com

Guild Of Ten, 19 Old Bridge St., Truro. Co-operative of craftsmen and women living in Cornwall. They seek to produce workmanship of the highest quality; knitwear, designer clothing, glass blowing, ceramics etc. Open M-Sa 9.30-5.30. (102/B4) guildof10.co.uk

Helen Feiler Gallery, 54 The Strand, Newlyn. Helen's a painter, print-maker and jeweller. She uses the lost-wax technique and her jewels are microcosms of the natural world. Open W Th & F 11-5 & By Appoint. 01736 330796 (107/G7) helenfeilergallery.com

Helland Bridge Pottery. Riverside home and studio of Paul and Rosie Jackson. A wide range of stunningly decorated hand-made pottery and garden sculpture. Fabulous water gardens. Open any time, but advised to call first. 01208 75240 (93/M10) paul-jackson.co.uk

Helland Bridge Pottery ss

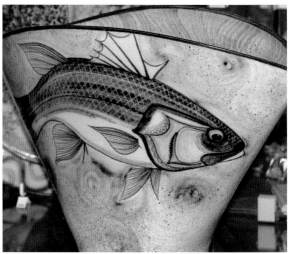

Adrian Brough Pottery

Kestle Barton, Manaccan, Helston. This is a new, community-based, arts centre with ever-changing exhibitions; painting, sculpture, ceramics, and events, all set within an ancient Cornish farmstead. Open Late Mar to Early Nov Tu-Sa 10.30-5. 01326 231811 (105/J3) kestlebarton.co.uk

Leach Pottery, Upper Stennack, St Ives. Founded by Bernard Leach (d.1979) and Shoji Hamada in 1920, and arguably the most influential studio pottery in the world. A living tribute to Bernard Leach and his legacy. Open daily, all year from 10, Su from 11. (107/K1) leachpottery.com

New Craftsman, 24 Fore St., St Ives. British Crafts Council Awards gallery celebrating 50+ years in business features ceramics, jewellery, glass, metalwork, and more. Open M-Sa 10-5. (107/K1) newcraftsmanstives.com

Prindl Pottery, Nr Lanhydrock. Japanese inspired pots; some are of enormous size and originality. Others are simply shaped in stoneware or porcelain. Open M-F 10-5, W/ Es by appointment. (100/C3) prindlpottery.co.uk

You May Also Like to Consider:

St Ives Ceramics, Lower Fish St. Collections of high quality ceramics. Work by John Bedding, Clive Bowen, Bernard Leach and Japanese artists from Mashiko. Open daily 10-5. (107/K1) st-ives-ceramics.co.uk

Trelissick Gallery. This is set within the National Trust's garden, and is run in partnership with the Cornwall Crafts Association to show off the best of Cornwall's arts and crafts. Open Feb-Dec M-Sa 10.30-5.30. (102/B6) trelissickgallery.co.uk

Trelowarren Gallery. Original home of the Cornwall Crafts Association, now regularly holds members and touring exhibitions. Open Mar- Nov. (105/H4) cornwallcrafts.co.uk

Penwith Gallery, St Ives ss

Barbara Hepworth Museum & Sculpture Garden, Barnoon Hill, St Ives. The house, studio, sculpture garden and workshop of the late Sculptress. 40 sculptures, paintings and photographs. 01736 796226. Open all year Tu-Su 10-4.20 and daily Mar-Oct 10-5.20. (107/K1) tate.org.uk/stives/hepworth

Bodmin Museum, Mount Folly. Exhibits of local history, Victorian Kitchen. 'Echoes of Bodmin Moor!'. 01208 77067. Open mid-Apr to Sept M-F 10.30-4.30 (Sa 2.30), Oct 10.30-2.30. (100/C1)

Bodmin - Duke of Cornwall's Light Infantry Museum, The Keep. Weapons, medals, uniforms, badges and military history based on the Duke of Cornwall's Light Infantry. Open Mar-Nov Tu-Su 10-5, Dec-Feb W-Sa 10-4.30. (100/C1) cornwalls-regimentalmuseum.org

Falmouth - National Maritime Museum, Discovery Quay. Historic collection of British and international boats. Designed "To promote an understanding of boats and their place in people's lives, to inspire new boat design and to promote an understanding of the maritime heritage of Cornwall." 01326 313388. Open daily 10-5. (99/M10) nmmc.co.uk

Falmouth Art Gallery, The Moor. Maritime pictures and quality temporary exhibitions. Works by Alfred Munnings, Frank Brangwyn, J W Waterhouse and Henry Scott Tuke. Open all year M-Sa 10-5. (99/M9) falmouthartgallery.com

Helston Folk Museum. Exhibits of rural life, crafts and industries of Helston and the Lizard which flourished in the C19 and C20s. Open all year M-Sa 10-4. (104/E2) museumofcornishlife.co.uk

Newlyn Art Gallery, New Road. An enterprising, and at times, shocking art venue with changing exhibitions of painting, sculpture, drawing and photography. Installation and esoteric space is a concept practiced with panache, and endearment. Gallery shop. Open daily M-Sa 10-5. (107/G7) newlynartgallery.co.uk

Penzance - Penlee House Gallery & Museum, Morrab Road. Paintings by the Newlyn School of Artists, plus social history and archaeology. Open daily M-Sa Apr-Oct 10-5, Nov-Mar 10-4.30. (107/G6) penleehouse.org.uk

Entrance to Tate St Ives

Porchcurno Telegraph Museum. The site of the first undersea cable laid in 1870 that became the world's largest and busiest submarine telegraph station. Thereafter, 14 cables linked Porthcurno to the British Empire employing a binary code, the forerunner of the internet. Sculpture garden and picnic areas. Open Apr-Oct daily 10-5, Nov-Mar W/Es & M 10.30-4. 01736 810966 (106/C10) telegraphmuseum.org.uk

Tate St Ives, Porthmeor Beach. Now with an impressive new extension. This is the first port-of-call for thousands who visit St Ives. They wish to walk in the shadow of Art and all its finery and pretension. Here you will discover displays of contemporary work in all variety of media. There are some very fine sculptures by Hepworth and a comprehensive show of St Ives' famous son, Alfred Wallis, fisherman and scrap merchant who didn't paint until he was 70! Worth a journey just for the view from the coffee shop and a visit to the bookshop. 01736 796226. Open daily 10-5.20. (107/K1) tate.org.uk/stives

You May Also Like to Consider:

The Exchange, Princes St., Penzance. Developed in conjunction with the Newlyn Art Gallery, this gallery showcases international art forms (sic), and holds regular educational programmes. Coffee shop. Open M-Sa 10-5. (107/H6) newlynartgallery.co.uk

Truro - Royal Cornwall Museum, River Street. World-famous collection of minerals, archaeology, ceramics, paintings and Old Master drawings. Archives and ephemera relating to Cornwall and the South West with extensive collection of photographs from 1845. Open Tu-Sa 10-4.45 01872 272205 (102/B4) royalcornwallmuseum.org.uk

Royal Cornwall Museum, Truro

Geevor Tin Mine ss

The Cornish landscape is haunted by silhouettes of chimneys and engine houses on the skyline, and by ramshackle desolate buildings beside the road. The remains of a once prosperous tin and copper mining industry. Most examples to be found in the Camborne to Redruth area, and on the Penwith Peninsula. Restored by the National Trust and other bodies. They stand in spectacular positions, and are worthy of a visit. The better known are: Wheal Coates, Engine House, Nr St Agnes and, Wheal Prosper Copper Mine, Nr Porthleven. Please Note: In areas of former mining activity, it is imperative that one keeps to the evident pathways. Walkers and their dogs have been known to disappear down hidden shafts.

Blue Hills Tin Streams.

Generations of miners have applied their trade here, from mining the valley floor, to tunnelling into the hillside. Guided tours of the skills of the ancient tinner; from rock to metal. Giftware. Open mid- Apr to mid-Oct Tu-Sa 10-2. 01872 553341 (97/B10) cornishtin.com

Botallack Engine Houses - The Crowns.

The haunting and terrifying remains of the famous tin mine, operational from 1720-1914, which employed 500 people. Tunnels and galleries were projected beneath the sea. The roaring Atlantic clearly audible above the miners' heads. In 1893 the roof collapsed drowning 29 men, 500 feet down, never to be recovered. NB Please keep to paths. (106/B5) trevithick-society.org.uk

Delabole - Slate Quarry.

1 1/2 mile circumference at depth of 500ft, 375 million years of geological history. Worked continuously since the C16 possibly by the Romans. Tours of Quarry from May-Aug, M-F at 2pm. 01840 212242 (93/M4) delaboleslate.co.uk

Dolcoath Mine.

At 3,500 ft below the surface, Cornwall's deepest mine. Shut down in 1921 following the tin slump after WW1. (98/E6)

Geevor Tin Mining Heritage Centre.

Set within the largest preserved mining site in the UK. A working mine until 1990, now a museum with tours of the surface plant and underground (12 & 2pm). Museum, film show, café and shop. Open Su-F from 9, underground tours from 10, 11, 13.00 & 1500 hrs, last admission in summer 4, in winter 3. 01736 788662 (106/B4) geevor.com

Gwennap Pit, Near St Day.

This amphitheatre was created by mining subsidence or divine intervention (depending on your point of view). It was landscaped in 1803 to fine tune excellent acoustics and is known as the Methodist 'Cathedral'. John Wesley first preached here in 1762 and in 1773 to a congregation of 32,000! Annual Methodist Meeting - spring

Poldark Mine ss

BHM. Visitor Centre open Spring BH M to 30 Sept M-F 10-4.30, Sa 10-1. (99/H5) gwennappit.co.uk

Huel Vor. Cornish for 'Great Work'. A disused mine with 30 foot wide seams worked at depths of 2,500 ft. (104/B1)

King Edward Mine Museum, Troon. Cornwall's industrial past revealed - the Portreath Tramroad, 11km and Great Flat Lode trails, 10km. Interpretation Centre. Croust Hut Café open all year. 01209 614681. Museum open East to Oct Tu-Sa 10-4, Su 1-4. (98/F6) kingedwardmine.co.uk

Poldark Mine. A World Heritage Site where you can follow in the footsteps of C18 tin miners along underground passages with easy, and difficult routes. Suitable for the elderly, the fit and fearless. Poldark Museum and film. Surface fun for the family. Open East, then all year 10-5.30. 01326 573173 (98/F10) poldarkmine.org.uk

Tregonning Hill. William Cookworthy, a Plymouth chemist discovered Kaolin here in 1768, a substance which is the basis of England's porcelain industry. Later, extensive finds were discovered around Hensbarrow Downs. St Austell grew to become the centre of the industry. Kaolin is a product of changed granite; the rock is extracted from enormous pits, 300ft deep and 1/2 mile across. Only a portion is utilised, the remainder is piled in great white heaps, hundreds of feet high like towering snow mountains, the 'Cornish Alps' on which vegetation scarcely grows (unless the Alp is part of the Eden Project). (104/C1)

Salmon fishing, Cotehele Quay ss

RAIL & INDUSTRIAL INTEREST

Bodmin & Wenford Railway ss

Bodmin & Wenford Railway, Bodmin General Station. Step back into the nostalgic 1940s with a 13-mile round trip on a standard gauge steam railway through the beautiful Cornish countryside. Trains services run from February to October. Details: website. 01208 73666 (100/C1) bodminrailway.co.uk

Bude's Old Canal. Built in 1819-26 at a length of 43 miles (61km). For 60 years used to transport coal and lime inland and to export grain and slate. Killed off by other railways. Best sections are at Marhamchurch, Hobbacott Down and Werrington. (91/G1) bude-canal.co.uk

Calstock Viaduct. 12-arch viaduct built to carry railway wagons from local mines to Calstock Quay. Whereby the wagons were raised and lowered in a lift. (83/J10)

Carnglaze Slate Caverns & The Rum Store. Famous subterranean lake with crystal clear blue-green water in three huge underground chambers of cathedral-like proportions. Guided tours. Rock and classical music concerts. Open all year M-Sa 10-5 (-8 Aug) 01579 320251 (101/H1) carnglaze.com

Cornish Gold & Pearl, Tolgus Mill. Craftsmen at work plus large jewellery exhibition. Weigh yourself in gold. Tin mining display and restaurant. Open all year M-Sa 9.30-5.30, Su 10.30-4.30. 01209 203280 (98/F4) cornwall-gold.com

Cotehele Quay (NT). Picturesque C18 and C19 buildings beside the River Tamar. A small out-station of the National Maritime Museum and berth for the restored Tamar sailing barge, 'Shamrock', a 57 foot ketch rigged vessel that plied its trade hereabouts in times gone by and you can board it on Sundays. Discovery Centre, Art and craft gallery and Edgcumbe tearoom. Open daily Apr-Oct. Canoe trips and Gig Club meet here. nationaltrust.org.uk

Goonhilly Earth Station. This is a new company achieving success winning contracts with all of the major satellite operators and working with 14 different universities. With plans to develop private Deep Space Communications and a mission to the moon with partners SSTL, ESA, the UK Space Agency and NASA. Visitor Centre no longer open. (105/H5) goonhily.org

Lappa Valley Railway & Leisure Park. Enjoy a two-mile return trip along a 15' gauge line to a pleasure area with boating lakes, crazy golf, maze, children's railway, walks and film show. Café and gift shop. Open daily East-Oct & 1/2 term 10.30-5.30. Train departs every 40 mins from 10.40 to 3.20. 01872 510317 (94/C7) lappavalley.co.uk

Launceston Steam Railway. Two-foot gauge steam railway using Victorian Locomotives along a beautiful country line. After 2 1/2 miles, Newmills Station, access to farm park. Transport and Industrial Museum with working exhibits. Café, shop and bookshop. Open East week, Spring BH & Oct 1/2 term, June Su-Th, July-Sept Su-F, 10.30-4.30. 01566 775665 (82/D2) launcestonsr.co.uk

Marconi Monument. The first transatlantic Morse Code messages were transmitted from this spot on 12 December 1901, and picked up by Gugliemo Marconi in St Johns, Newfoundland. (104/E6)

You May Also Like to Consider:

Royal Albert Bridge, Saltash. This beautiful, "Bowstring Suspension Bridge" is an iron single-track railway bridge built by I K Brunel in 1859. His last great feat of engineering. The design comprises of a wrought iron tubular arch or bow in the form of a parabola in a combination with sets of suspension chains hanging on each side of the tube in a catenary curve. (87/J5) royalalbertbridge.co.uk

St Austell Brewery Visitor Centre & Hicks Bar. Traditional brewers for 140 years. Guided tours and beer sampling at 11am and 4pm. Licensed shop. Open M-Sa 9-5.30. 01726 66022 (100/A8) staustellbrewery.co.uk

Wheal Martyn China Clay Country Park, Nr St Austell. Mining and Heritage Centre. Work Horse to War Horse, open air displays, historic nature trails with spectacular views of modern clay pit. Children's challenge trail, licensed café and shop. Dog friendly. Open daily mid-Jan to 23 Dec 10-5. 01726 850362 (95/K8) wheal-martyn.com

World of Model Railways, Mevagissey. 2,000 + models and 30 trains controlled in sequence. Shop. Open daily late Mar to Oct & winter W/Es, 10-5 & winter W/Es 12-4. 01726 842457 (103/L4) model-railway.co.uk

Prince Albert Bridge, Saltash

Cornish Day Sailing, North Quay, Falmouth.
Sail around Falmouth Bay on a 47ft Ketch, enjoy a Cornish Crab deli lunch and cream tea from 9-4pm or try a sunset sail from 6-9pm. 01326 212320 (102/A10) cornishdaysailing.com

Extreme Academy, Watergate Bay.
"A ski resort on a beach" were the founders intent. And, still aimed at family, sporting activities: surfing, paddle surfing going on to host top-level kite surf events and powerboat racing. Hot showers and changing facilities. 01637 860840 (94/C3) extremeacademy.co.uk

Falmouth School of Sailing, Boat Park Grove Place.
Courses range from dinghy, to keelboat, to powerboats, taking you to varying levels of seamanship. 01326 211311 (102/A10) falmouthschoolofsailing.co.uk

Fistral Beach Surf School, Fistral Beach Complex. Newquay.
Lessons for families, groups and individuals at the home of British surfing. Open all year. Equipment included in fee. Parking available. 01637 850737 (94/A5) fistralbeachsurfschool.co.uk

Gwithian Academy of Surfing. 1 Godrevy Towans.
A great place to start this tricky sport. Open from April to end October for beginner and improver surfing courses. Private and group lessons. Accommodation. 01736 757579 (98/A5) surfacademy.co.uk

Lizard Adventure, The Lizard.
Fancy some exploration and wetsuit thrills? Try bushcraft, coasteering, kayaking, suping (paddle boarding), rock climbing. Open all year. 07845 204040 lizardadventure.co.uk

Mylor Boat Hire, Mylor Yacht Harbour.
A variety of craft are available to hire: Cornish Shrimpers, Sailing Picarooners to motor launches and kayaks/SUPS. 01326 377745 (102/A8) mylorboathire.co.uk

Outdoor Adventures, Atlantic Court, Bude.
Activity centre for the ultimate coastal experience: coasteering, surfing, coastal traversing, sea cliff abseils, rock climbing, sea kayaking. Activity Weekends. Accommodation. Tuition. 01288 362900 (90/F5) outdooradventure.co.uk

Cornish Day Sailiong ss

Lizard Adventures ss

Pinuccia, Hotel Tresanton.
This is a classical 1938 8 meter yacht designed by Vincenzo Vittorio Baglietto for Italy's entry in the Sailing World Cup and international competitions. Guests of the hotel may charter her from May to the end of September with Pinuccia's professional skipper. A champagne lunch is provided along with a fair wind and a steady course to the estuaries of the Helford and Fal rivers. (102/B9) tresanton.com

Sail Agnes, Penryn. Charter this 46 ft Pilot Cutter, and explore the Cornish Coast, Isles of Scilly, Brittany and beyond for day trips or weekly sojourns. 07790 638084 (103/A9) workingsail.co.uk

Saltair Adventures, Mylor Yacht Harbour. Coasteer, Climb/abseil, Sup, Kayak, Surf… all is available with experienced guides and team leaders. Bespoke activities available. They cater for Military, Stag/Hen parties, families and youth groups. 07828 246278 (102/A8) saltair.co.uk

Sennen Surfing Centre, Sennen Cove. Learn to surf or improve your skills in arguably the clearest water in England. Sennen is a surfing community of unrivalled expertise and this is one of England's longest running schools. All abilities are catered for. 01736 871227 (106/B8) sennensurfingcentre.co.uk

Outdoor Adventure, Bude ss

CYCLING TRAILS

Cycling Couple Cornwall

Bugle to the Eden Project, Nr St Austell. 6km/4miles. Crosses the heathlands of Treskilling Downs past woodland and lakes. (95/L7)

Camel Trail (NCN 3 & 32), Padstow. 27km/17miles. Cornwall's most popular trail with an estimated 500,000 annual visitors. Bodmin to Padstow with deviation north to Poley's Bridge. Also suitable for jogging, walking and bird watching. Cycle hire in Padstow and Wadebridge. Info on: 01872 327310. (92/D8)

Cardinham Woods, Nr Bodmin. 5km/3m. Circuit around woodland owned by the Forestry Commission. Also, 4-waymarked walks of 3-7.5km. Parking available. Café. (100/E1)

Coast to Coast Trail, Nr Truro. 17km/11miles. Park at the Bike Chain Bissoe Bike Hire. Connects two historic harbours, Portreath and Devoran and passes by wildlife and ancient woodland. (99/M6)

Great Flat Lode Trail, Nr Redruth. 12km/7miles. Park at the Mineral Tramway Centre. A circular route exploring the landscape of tin and copper mines from the 1860s. (99/H5)

Pentewan Trail, Nr St Austell. 6km/4miles. An easy off-road route from London Apprentice to Pentewan with an off-shoot to Heligan Gardens that uses 1/2 mile of road. Bike hire. (103/L3)

Portreath Branchline Trail, Nr Redruth. 9km/5miles. Connects to the Great Flat Lode Trail by using quiet roads. (98/E3)

Redruth & Chasewater Railway Trail. 12km/7miles. Park at Twelveheads. Based on the old railway lines. It is mostly off-road with some major roads to cross. (99/K5)

Tehidy Trail, Nr Redruth. 4km/2.5miles. Park in Portreath. Linear route using the tracks and trails through Tehidy Country Park. (98/E3)

Wheal Martyn to the Eden Project, Nr St Austell. 8km/5miles. Cycle through clay country, woodland and heathland with stunning views. Bike hire. (95/K8)

FUN & ADVENTURE

Arthurian Centre, Nr Camelford. Site of Arthurian legend and folk lore. Exhibition centre, woodland and river walks, tearoom and gift/bookshop. Play area. Open daily. 01840 213947 (84/E2) arthur-online.co.uk

Camel Creek Adventure Park, Nr Wadebridge. Mega-slides, twisters, water slides. Shire horses, farm museum with 120 acres to roam. Restaurant. 01841 540276. Open Spring W/Es, then daily Apr to early Nov 10-5. (95/G1) camelcreek.co.uk

Dairyland Farmworld. All-weather farm park with milking parlour, heritage centre, playground, nature trail and cream teas. Open daily Apr to Oct from 10 & School hols. 01872 510246 (94/D7) dairylandfarmworld.com

Flambards Experience, Helston. All-weather activities and attraction; Victorian Village and "Britain in the Blitz" experiences, Space Quest, live entertainment, Hands-On Science, Operation Sealion and much more. Open most days Early Apr to end Oct 10.30-5.(104/E3) flambards.co.uk

Hidden Valley Discovery Park, Nr Launceston. Adventure park and garden railway centre. Treasure hunts based around a shipwreck. Play area. Farm animals. Café. Two coarse fishing lakes. Open Apr-Sept Su-F & Aug Sa, 10.30-5.30. (82/A2) hiddenvalleydiscoverypark.co.uk

Land's End - The Natural Landscape. 5 Exhibitions including Arthur's Quest, Air Sea Rescue and End to End Story. Craft workshops. Bar/Hotel. 0870 4580044. Open all year 10-dusk. (106/A9) landsend-landmark.co.uk

Trethorne Leisure ss

Old MacDonalds Farm, Porthcothan Bay. Designed for younger children where they can feed the pets and enjoy pony rides, train rides, birds of prey, picnics, crazy golf, indoor play area and café. Camping. Open daily Apr-Oct 10-6. 01841 540829 (92/B10) oldmacdonalds.co.uk

Shire Horse Farm & Carriage Museum, Redruth. A visit will take you back in time to a working farm with 15 shire horses and a display of horse-drawn vehicles. Wheelright and Blacksmith's shop. Free wagon rides, cream teas. Open East-Oct Su-F 10-4. 01209 713606 (98/F7) shirehorseandcarriagemuseum.org.uk

Trethorne Leisure Park, Nr Launceston. Undercover family entertainment; milk a cow, bottle feed lambs, see chicks hatch. Ten pin bowling (open daily from 10), gladiator duels, drop-slide, astra-slide, restaurant, bar and shop. Farmhouse B&B. Open daily all year 10-6. 01566 86324 (82/B3) trethorneleisure.com

Waterworld, Leisure Centre, Newquay. Fun pool, gym, dance and aerobic studio, sauna, solarium. skate park. 01637 853828. Open daily. (94/A5) newquaywaterworld.co.uk

Sky Swinger at Flambards Theme Park ss

Minack Theatre ss

Falmouth – The Poly, 24 Church St. 200 seat theatre (cinema) holds music, theatre and dance. Four galleries put on changing exhibitions. Café/bar. Open M-Sa 10-5. 01326 319461 (99/M10) thepoly.org

Kneehigh Theatre Group, Walsingham Place, Truro. Through the conduit of The Asylum (a beautiful and nomadic structure), this group of players produce creative, thought provoking, challenging and joyful productions to tease and entertain their audience. 01872 267910 (102/B4) kneehigh.co.uk

Minack Open Air Theatre, Porthcurno. Theatre cut out of the cliff side with full season of plays, musicals and operas in a unique 750-seat theatre. Summer Season: May to mid-Sept. Exhibition Centre tells the story of Rowena Cade who built the theatre. Café with spectacular view. Open daily Apr to mid-Sept 10-5, winter from 10-dusk (closed 24/25 Dec). 01736 810694 (106/C10) minack.com

Newlyn Filmhouse, The Coombe. This is a fabulous little cinema with 2-screens converted from an old fish cellar and smokery. Matinees. Café/bar serve seriously good food. 01736 332222 (107/G7) newlynfilmhouse.com

St Neots - The Rum Store, Carnglaze Caverns. Classical and pop concerts put on in underground 400-seat auditorium. Superb acoustics. Caverns open M-Sa 10-5, (-8 Aug) 01579 320251 (101/H1) carnglaze.com

St Piran's Round, Perranporth. An ancient amphitheatre where plays were performed in the C17. (97/D8)

Sterts Arts & Environment Centre. Lively programme of dance, music and theatre. Family picnics ideal before performance. Gallery and Workshops. Café and Bar open for shows and Event Days. 01579 362382. Open daily (theatre June-Sept) except Su. (82/A8) sterts.co.uk

Swamp Circus, Lower Market Street, Penryn. The long-held ideal of this circus is to engage with you, the audience through their performance and their teaching projects. A number of workshops and camps are organised throughout the year. They also manage Cornwall's Circus School with events for families and children across Cornwall. Organic camp site for the hardy and rustic minded. 01326 377008 (99/M9) circokernow.co.uk

CALENDAR OF EVENTS

January
Wadebridge. North Cornwall Point to Point

February
St Columb. Cornish Hurling
St Ives Hurling the Silver Ball

March
Cotehele Daffodils Festival
Eden Bulb Mania
Liskeard Annual Art Exhibition
Mount Edgcumbe Camelia Collection
St Piran's Day

April
Boscastle Walking Week
Camborne Trevithick Day
Porthleven Food & Music Festival
St Endellion Music Festival

May
Cornish International Male Voice Choir Fest'
Falmouth Asparagus Festival
Fowey Daphne Du Maurier Festival of Arts & Literature
Helston Furry/Flora Dance
Launceston Steam & Vintage Rally
Newquay Longboard Championships
Padstow 'Obby Oss' Celebrations

June
Falmouth. Fal River Festival
Kernow Midsummer Bonfires
Liskeard Festival
Mevagissey Festival Week
Penzance. Golowan Festival
Polperro Festival
Saltash Town Regatta
St Keverne. An Gov Day
St Merryn Steam Rally
Wadebridge· Royal Cornwall Show

July
Boconnoc Steam Fair
Bodmin Riding & Heritage Day
InterCeltic Watersports Festival
Liskeard & District Agricultural Show
Looe Lions Carnival Week
Padstow Vintage Rally
Pendeen Band Week
Perranporth Carnival
Porthleven Lifeboat Day
Ruan Minor Vintage Car Rally
Rock Sailing Club. Shrimper Week
St Endellion Music

July (continued)
St Germans. Port Eliot Literary Fest'
St Mawes Regatta
Stithians Show
Tremough. Celtic Congress
Wadebridge Wheels

August
Bude Carnival
Bude Horticultural Show
Camel Sailing Week
Camelford Agricultural Show
Cornwall Folk Festival
Crying the Neck
Delabole Wind Fair
Falmouth Week
Fowey Royal Regatta & Carnival Week
Hayle Festival
Henri-Lloyd Falmouth Week
Mount Edgcumbe. Classic Car Rally
Morvah Pasty Day Festival
Morval Vintage Steam Rally
Newlyn Fish Festival
Newquay. Rip Curl Boardmasters
Padstow Carnival
Padstow Lifeboat Day
Polruan Regatta
St Agnes Festival
St Keverne Ox St Just Feast
Wadebridge Carnival

September
Bude Jazz Festival
Truro. Cornish Food & Drink Festival
Looe Valley Walking Festival
Penzance. Open Gorseth
St Ives Festival

October
Boscastle. Food, Arts & Crafts Festival
Falmouth Oyster Festival
Perranporth. Lowender Peran

November
Falmouth & Penryn. Cornwall Film Fest'
Looe Food Festival
Roseland Festival
Wadebridge Prime Stock Show

December
Padstow Christmas Festival
Mousehole. Tom Bawcock's Eve

For specific dates please contact the local Tourist Information Centre

MAPS OF CORNWALL: LEGEND

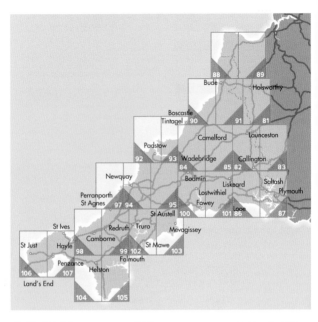

♙ Abbey/Cathedral	☎ Pub/Inn	⊕ Leisure/Sports Centre
✕ Battle Site	🚂 Railway Interest	⚓ Lifeboat
🏡 Bed & Breakfast Accomodation	✗ Restaurant	℗ Parking
☕ Café	🍴 Self Catering Accommodation	⏲ Picnic Site
🏰 Castle	⌸ Standing Stone/Barrow	⌂A Tents & Caravans
⛪ Church/Chapel of Interest	♕ Theatre/Concert Hall	⛵ Sailing
🎬 Cinema	🚻 Tourist Information	🏄 Surfing
♟ Craft Interest	✿ Tumulus/Tumuli	🅸 Tourist Information
✝ Cross	⚵ Viewpoint	🏄 Windsurfing
♻ Cycleway	✖ Windmill/Wind Farm	▲ Youth Hostel
🎡 Fun Park/Leisure Park	⊕ Airfield	🐄 Agricultural Interest
✳ Hill Fort/Ancient Settlement	⌒ Aquarium	♧ Arboretum
🏛 Historic Building	⛵ Boat Trips	☙ Bird Reserve
🏨 Hotel	Å Camping Site (Tents)	❀ Garden of Interest
🏭 Industrial Interest	⛺ Caravan Site	🍇 Vineyard
🛞 Karting	⅄⅄ Ferry (Pedestrians)	🐾 Walks/Nature Trails
⚑ Lighthouse	⇌ Ferry (Vehicles)	⅄ Wildlife Park
⛏ Mining Interest/Engine Houses	⌁ Fishing Trips	🐘 Zoo
☆ Miscellaneous/Natural Attraction	⌖ 9/18 Hole Golf Course	℗ National Trust Car Park
⌂ Museum/Art Gallery	⚓ Harbour	
☕ Pottery	⚓ Inshore Rescue Boat	

▬▬▬	A Road
▬▬▬	B Road
─────	Minor Road
- - - - -	Other Road or Track (not necessarily with public or vehicular access)
●━━━━●	Railway
·············	Cycleway

381m.
305m.
229m.
152m
76m.

Open Space owned by the National Trust

Built-up Area

Scale 1:100,000

```
0                1        (miles)    2

0        1        2        (km)
```

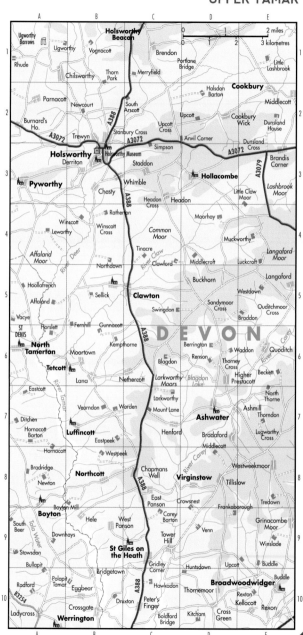

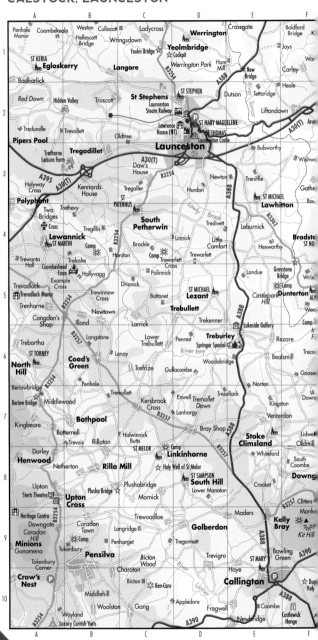

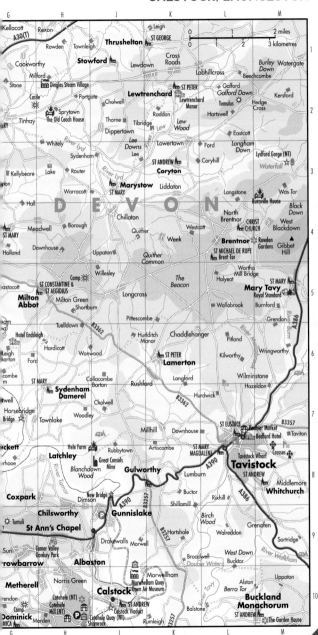

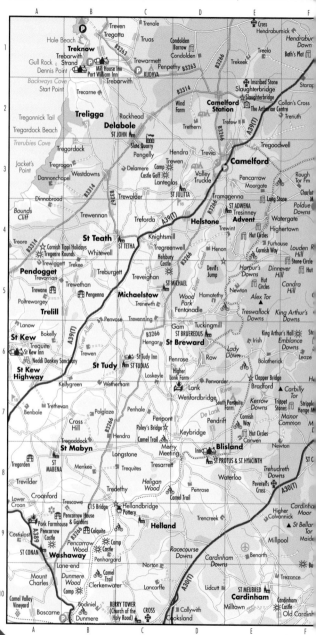

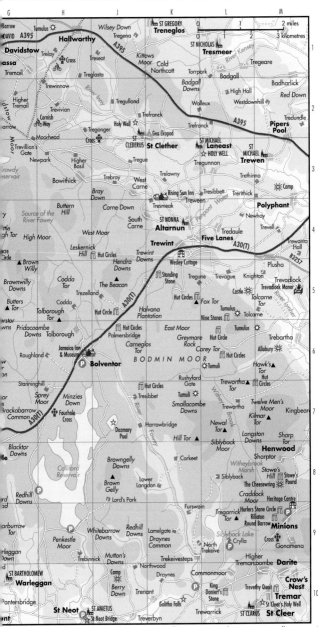

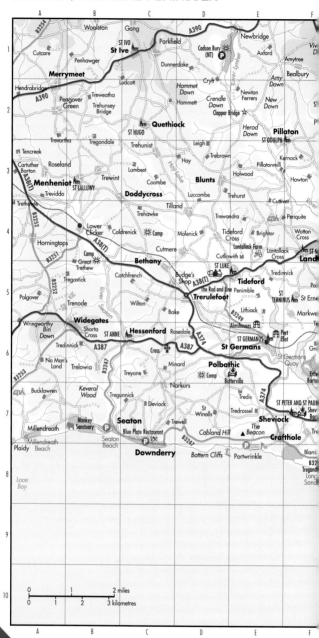

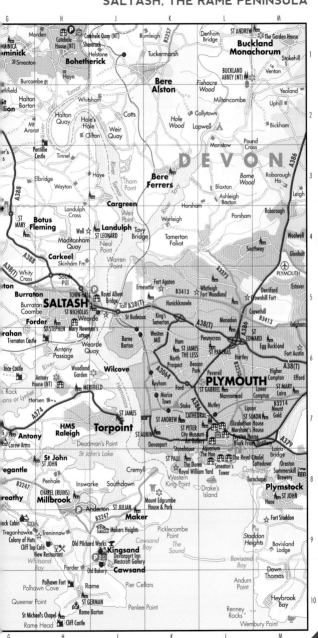

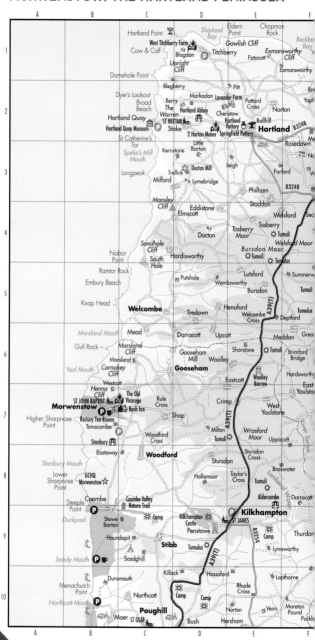

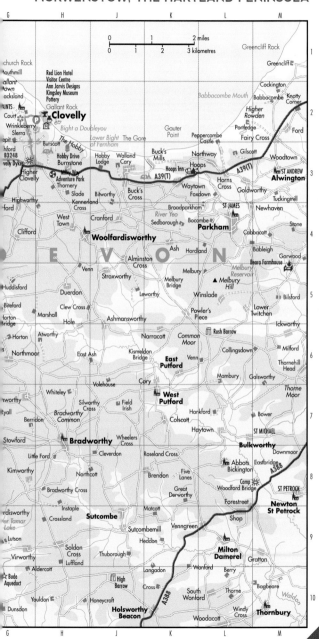

G   H   J   K   L   M

0   1   2 miles
0   1   2   3 kilometres

Greencliff Rock

1

church Rock
Mouthmill
Gallant
town
ackland
SAINTS
Court
Wrinkleberry
Sierra
apit
hford
B3248
velly Dykes

Red Lion Hotel
Visitor Centre
Ann Jarvis Designs
Kingsley Museum
Pottery
Gallant Rock

Clovelly

Greencliff

Cockington

Babbacombe Mouth

Babbacombe

Knotty
Corner

2

Bight a Doubleyou
Lower Bight
of Fernham

The Gore

Gauter
Point

Peppercombe
Castle

Higher
Rowden

Portledge

Fairy Cross

Ford

Burscott
Hobby Drive
Burnstone

The Hobby

Higher
Clovelly

Highworthy
ford

Milky Way
Adventure Park
Thornery
Slade

Hobby
Lodge

Walland
Cary

Buck's
Mills

Northway

Hoops Inn
Hoops

A39(T)

Waytown
Foxdown

Horns
Cross

Gilscott

Woodtown

ST ANDREW
Alwington

Goldworthy

Tuckingmill

3

West
Town

Bitworthy
Kennerland
Cross

Buck's
Cross

Broadparkham
Sedborough

ST JAMES
Parkham

Bocombe
Cabbacott

Newhaven

Stone

4

Clifford

Cranford

River Yeo

Woolfardisworthy

Ash

Hordland

Bableigh

Gorwood

D   E   V   O   N

Venn

Almington
Cross

Stroxworthy

Melbury
Bridge

Melbury

Melbury
Hill

Melbury
Reservoir

Beara Farmhouse

5

Huddisford

Duerdon

Lew
orthy

Winslade

Lower
Twitchen

Bilsford

Biteford
orton
Bridge

Clew Cross
Marshall

Hole

Ashmansworthy

Powler's
Piece

Ickworthy

Horton

Atworthy

Narracott

Common
Moor

Rush Barrow

6

Northmoor

East Ash

Kismeldon
Bridge

Venn

Collingsdown

Milford

Thornehill
Head

Whiteley

Volehouse

Cory

**East
Putford**

Mambury

Galsworthy

Thorne
Moor

7

worthy

yall

Berridon

Silworthy
Cross

Bradworthy
Common

Field
Irish

**West
Putford**

Hankford

Colscott

Bower

Stowford

Bradworthy

Wheelers
Cross

Haytown

ST MICHAEL
Bulkworthy

Downmoor

8

Little Ford

Cleverdon

Roseland Cross

Abbots
Bickington

Eastbridge

A388

Kimworthy

Northcott

Brendon

Five
Lanes

Camp
Woodford Bridge

ST PETROCK

Bradworthy Cross

Great
Derworthy

Forestreet

**Newton
St Petrock**

9

rdisworthy
er Tamar
Lake

Instaple
Crossland

Sutcombe

Matcott

Sutcombemill

Shop

Lutson

Soldon
Cross

Heddon

Thuborough

Venngreen

10

Virworthy

Aldercott

Luffland

Langadon

Wonford

Berry

**Milton
Damerel**

Gratton

Bagbeare

Bude
Aqueduct

Youldon

Honeycroft

High
Barrow

Cross

A388

South
Wonford

Thorne

Windy
Cross

Waldon

Thornbury

Dunsdon

**Holsworthy
Beacon**

Woodacott

G   H   J   K   L   M

0   1   2 miles
0   1   2   3 kilometres

Wanson
Foxhole Po
Millook Haven
Outdoor Adventure
Cancleave Strand   Millool
Dizzard Point   Commo
Chipman Strand   Trebar
                                                    Cornish
                                                    Way
                                            Dizzard
                                      Tresmorn   Trengay
Pencannow   Camp   Trewir
Point   St Gennys   Treworgie
              ST GENESIUS
Bray's Point   P   Coxford
Cambeak   Crackington
                          Haven
                                      Rosecare
Little Strand   Hallagather
The Strangles   Wainhouse
            Trevigue   Crackington   Corner
Voter Run
          Trevigue Wildlife Conservation   Ro
Rusey Beach   High   Baypark
               Cliff   Pengold
                      Camp   Pencuke
          Buckator   Round
Beeny Sisters Gull Rock P Newton   Hayes
Fire Deacon Point   Tresparrett   Tumu
                  Camp   Posts   B3263   Tre
Pentargon   Ringford   Collamoo
                          Tresparrett Cansford Head
              Beeny Trebyla B3263 Downs   Trevillia
Penally Point (NT) Farm Shop & Cafe   Marshgate Cocksport Cornish
      Wilapark (NT) Museum of Witchcraft Tresparrett   Way
Short   The Old Parsonage ST JULIOT'S Hennett   Cardew
Long Island Napoleon Inn Valency The Old Rectory Trevilla
Island Boscastle Bottreaux Valley (NT) R. Valency   Mill
Trevalga ST SYMPHORIAN'S Castle Treworld   ST DENIS
    Cross ST PETROCK MINSTER Lesnewth Trevilla Otterham
Trethevey   ST MICHAEL Helset Down Otterham Roose Trela
    Polrunny B3266 Tredorne Tregrylls   Down
Trethevey   Hallgarden
St Nectan's Glen Reddivallen   Otterham
Halgabron Waterfall & Chapel Vendown Hallwell Station   Tregray
    St Nectan's   Cross   Tumuli   Tumuli
    Kieve Waterpit   Tich Barrow
Trenale   Down Hendraburnick   Tumuli   Hallw

A   B   C   D   E   F

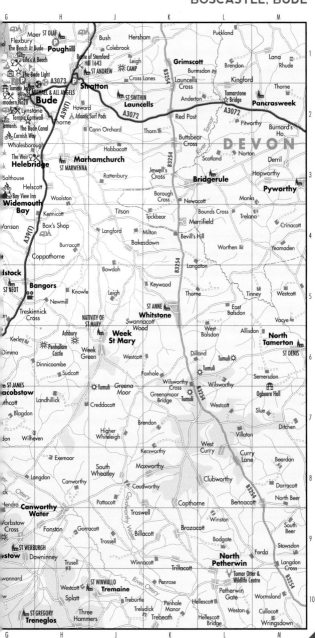

Maer ST OLAF
Flexbury
The Beach At Bude
Life's A Beach
Poughill
Bush
Hersham
Colebrook
Puckland
Lana
Rhude
The Bude Light
Tommy Jack's
A3073
modern 3028
ST MICHAEL & ALL ANGELS
Bude
Battle of Stamford
Hill 1643
ST ANDREW
Leigh
CAMP
Grimscott
Burmsdon
Brendon
Kingford
Thorne
Cross Lanes
Launcells
Cross
Howard
Atlantic Surf Pods
Lynstone
Temple Cornwall
Stratton
ST SWITHIN
Launcells
A3072
Anderton
Tamarstone
Bridge
A3072
Pancrasweek
Red Post
Pitworthy
Burnard's
Ho.
Thorne
Cann Orchard
Thorn
Buttsbear
Cross
DEVON
Whalesborough
The Weir
Helebridge
ST MARWENNA
Hobbacott
Marhamchurch
Jewell's
Cross
Scotland
Norton
Derril
Salthouse
Helscott
Bay View Inn
**Widemouth
Bay**
Woolston
Rattenbury
Borough
Cross
Newcastle
Bridgerule
Hopworthy
Monks
Pyworthy
Kennicott
Box's Shop
Titson
Tackbeck
Bounds Cross
Merrifield
Trelana
Crinacott
Burracott
Langford
Milton
Bevill's Hill
Worthen
Yeomaden
Coppathorne
Bakesdown
Bowdah
Langaton
Bangors
ST NEOT
Knowle
Newmill
Leigh
Keywood
Thorne
Tinney
Westcott
Treskinnick
Cross
NATIVITY OF
ST MARY
Swannacott
Wood
ST ANNE
Whitstone
East
Balsdon
Vacye
Kerley
Ashbury
Penhallam
Castle
**Week
St Mary**
West
Balsdon
Allisdon
**North
Tamerton**
Dimma
Dinnicoombe
Sudcott
Week
Green
Westcott
Dilland
Tumuli
Tumuli
ST DENIS
ST JAMES
Jacobstow
Northcott
Landhillick
Tumuli
Greena
Moor
Creddacott
Foxhole
Wilsworthy
Cross
Greenamoor
Bridge
Tumuli
Wilsworthy
Westcott
Semersdon
Ogbeare Hall
Slue
Blagdon
Wilheven
Higher
Whiteleigh
Brendon
West
Curry
Villaton
Ditchen
Exemoor
Kersworthy
Maxworthy
Curry
Lane
Beardan
Langdon
South
Wheatley
Canworthy
Caudworthy
Clubworthy
Darracott
North Beer
**Canworthy
Water**
Warbstow
Cross
Fonston
Pattacott
Troswell
Copthorne
Bennacott
Gorracott
Billacott
Brazacott
Winston
Bodgate
South
Beer
Stowsdon
ST WERBURGH
Warbstow
Downinney
Trusell
Trossell
Winnacott
Trillacott
**North
Petherwin**
Forda
Langdon
Cross
Wonnard
Westcott
Splatt
ST WINWALLO
Tremaine
River Ottery
Penrose
Treburtle
Penhale
Manor
Hellescott
Tamar Otter &
Wildlife Centre
Petherwin
Gate
Wormsland
ST GREGORY
Treneglos
Three
Hammers
Treludick
Trebeath
Hellescott
Bridge
Weston
Cullacott
Wringsdown

A B C D E F

1

2

0   1   2 miles
0   1   2   3 kilometres

3

4

5

The Mouls

Newland   Rumps Point

Pentire Point   Corn Hea

Pentire

New Polzeath

Hayle Bay

Padstow Bay   The Wate

Crams   Stepper Point   Polzea

Butter Hole   Mowhay Café   Trebethe

St Moritz Hotel

Gunver Head   Daymer Bay   Trewiston

Lellisick   Brea Hill ▲ ST ENODOC   Pit

Merope Rocks   Porthmissen Bridge   Crugmeer   Rock

Trevose Head   Mother Ivey's Bay   Tregirls   St Enodoc Bar & Hotel

Quies   Dinas Head   Mother Ivey Cottage   Harlyn Bay   Porthmissen   Prideaux Place

Trevose   Trethillick   Farm Shop

Booby's Bay   Ancient Burial Ground   Trevone   Treator   Porthilly Cove   Stoptic

St Constantine's Chapel   Harlyn   Windmill   Padstow Museum   Porthilly

Constantine Bay   Padstow

Rick Stein's Café

Treyarnon Bay   Constantine Bay   Seafood Restaurant   National Lobster Hatchery

Cornish Arms   ST MERRYN   St Petroc's Hotel   Dinas

Towan   No6 Restaurant   Treyarnon   St Merryn   Prawn On The Lawn   Tregonce   Camel Trail

Pepper Cove   Shop Trehemborne   Tregavone   Trevarrick   Halwyn

Fox Cove   Carnevas   Trevean   Rosken   Molesworth Manor   Burgois

Minnows Islands   Cornish Way   Roscullion   Tregonna   ST PETROCK

Porthcothan Beach   Trescore Islands   Porthcothan   Old Macdonald's Farm   The Old Mill House   ST IDA   Trevance

Porth Mear   Little Petherick   Mellingey   St Issey   Trewince

Park Head   Tumuli   Pentire   Trevemedar   Treburrick   Penrose   Trenance   Ha

A B C D E F

Long Island

The Sisters
Willapark

Lye Rock

Barras Nose
Tintagel Castle
The Island
Tintagel Head

Trethevey
Bossiney
St Nectan's Glen

Tintagel
The Old Post Office (NT)
King Arthur's Great Halls
Visitor Centre

ST MATERIANA

Tintagel
Treven
Trenale
Tregatta

Halgabron

Dunderhole Point

Glebe
Cliff

Truas

Hole Beach

Treknow
Trebarwith
Strand

B3263

Trewarmett

Gull Rock
Dennis Point

Mill House Inn
Port William Inn

Trebarwith
KUDHVA

Backways Cove
Start Point

Tregonnick Tail

Trecarne

Tregardock Beach

Treligga

Rockhead

Delabole
ST JOHN

Trerubies Cove

Tregardock

Slate Quarry
Pengelly

Jacket's Point

Tregagon

Westdowns

Delamere

PORT ISAAC
Nathan Outlaw
The Old School House
The Slipway Hotel
Varley Head

Port Isaac Bay

Delabole Point
Ranie Point

Dannonchapel

B3314

Trewalder

B3267

Port Isaac
Roscarrock

Tresungers
Point
ST PETER

Dinnabroad

Trewennan

Kellan
Head

Scarnor
Point

Bounds Cliff

Knightsmill

Portquin

Trefreock
Pottery

Trewetha
Cellars

Treore

B3314

Tregeare Rounds

St Teath
ST TETHA
Tregrenner
Whitewell

Longcross
Victorian
Garden
Wave 7 Studio

Cross Shaft

Trelights

Tresungers

Pendoggett

Trewiggett
Trevorrian

Cornish Tipi Holidays

Trekee

Treburgett

Treveighan

Treviglan

ST ENDELLIENTA

Trewane

Trewethan

B3314

Plain Street

St Endellion

Treharrock

Poltreworgey

Pengenna

Gunvenna

Trevathan Farm
Trevathan

Trentinney

Pennytinney

Trelill

Penvose

St Minver

Tregellist

Lanow

Bokelly

Tregwarmond

Trewethern

ST JAMES

Trequite

River Allen

Trewen

St Tudy Inn

St Tudy
ST TUDIAS

zzick

Trevine

Rooke

Pellengarrow

Blakes
Keiro
Old Windmill

Tredower

Maltsters
Arms

**Chapel
Amble**

St Kew

Kellygreen

Wetherham

**St Kew
Highway**

Lower
Amble

River Amble

Dinham
Trewornan Manor

Trewornan

Tregorden

Kelly

Trethevan

Benbole

B3266

Palglaze

Penhale

Cross
Hill

Tregunna
Camel Trail
Trevanson

Burniere

Bodieve

Castle Killibury

Three Holes
Cross

Tregaddock

Hendra

St Mabyn

Longstone

B3266

ecross
St Breock
showground
ST BREOCK

A39(T)
C15 Bridge

Trenant
ST CONAN

Egloshayle

Trevarner

Tregarden

ST
MABENA

Menkee

Trequites

cribed
tone

Polmorla

Wadebridge
Eglos Pottery

Clapper
Sladesbridge

Trevilder

Croanford

Tredethy

C15 Bridge

Hellandbridge
Pottery

Nanscow

Treneague

Treraven

Pendavey

Lower
Croan

Park

Tredannick

Pencarrow House
& Gardens

Trescowe

Helland

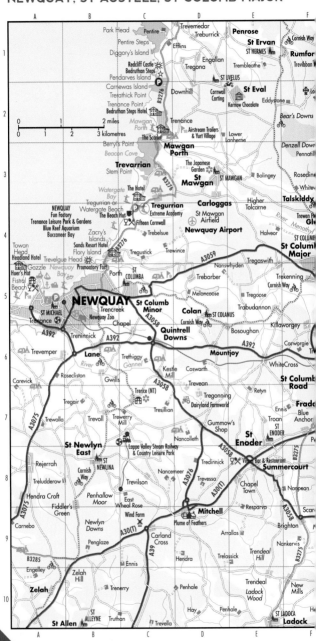

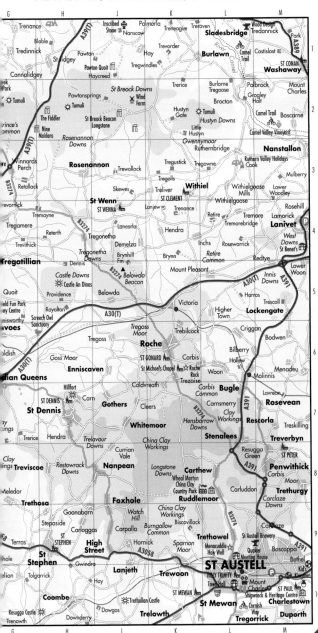

Wheal Coates Engine House, St Agnes

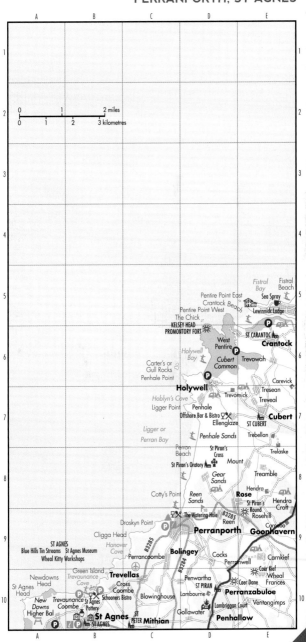

A B C D E

0   1   2 miles
0 1   2   3 kilometres

Fistral Bay
Fistral Beach
Pentire Point East
Crantock Beach
Sea Spray
Pentire Point West
Lewinnick Lodge
The Chick
KELSEY HEAD
PROMONTORY FORT
West Pentire
ST CARANTOC
Crantock
Holywell Bay
Carter's or Gull Rocks
Penhale Point
Cubert Common
Trevowah
Hoblyn's Cove
Trevornick
Carevick
Tresean
Treveal
Ligger Point
Penhale
Offshore Bar & Bistro
Ellenglaze
ST CUBERT
Cubert
Trebellan
Ligger or Perran Bay
Penhale Sands
Trelaske
Perran Beach
St Piran's Cross
Mount
St Piran's Oratory
Gear Sands
Treamble
Cotty's Point
Reen Sands
Hendra
Rose
Hendra Croft
St Piran's Round
Rosehill
Droskyn Point
The Watering Hole
Reen
Perranporth
Goonhavern
Cligga Head
Hanover Cove
Bolingey
Cocks
Perranwell
Carnkief
ST AGNES
Blue Hills Tin Streams St Agnes Museum
Wheal Kitty Workshops
Perrancoombe
Caer Kief
Wheal Frances
Newdowns Head
Green Island
Trevaunance Cove
Trevellas
Penwartha
ST PIRAN
Caer Dane
St Agnes Head
Cross Coombe
Schooners Bistro
Blowinghouse
Lambourne
Perranzabuloe
Ventongimps
New Downs
Trevaunance Coombe
St Agnes Pottery
St Agnes
ST PETER
Mithian
Gollawater
Lambriggan Court
Penhallow
Higher Bal

A B C D E

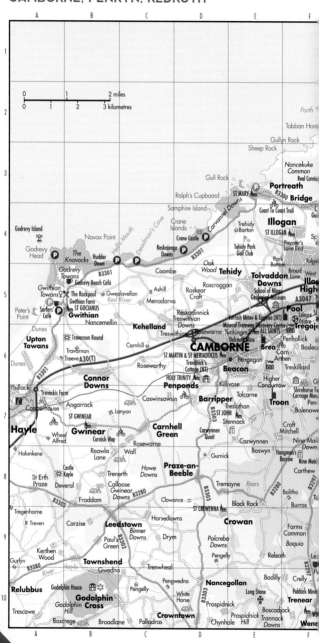

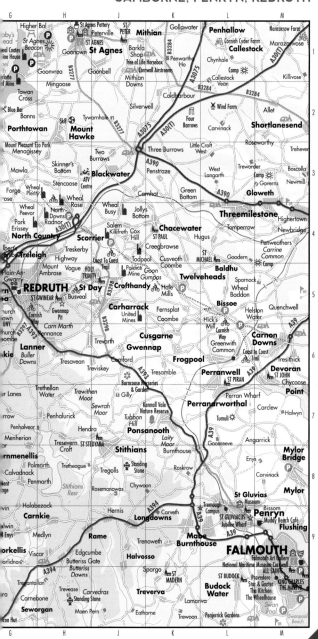

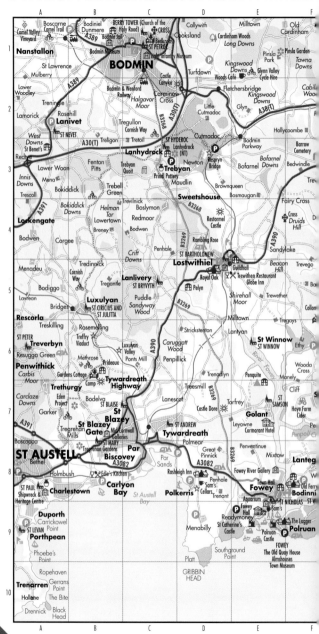

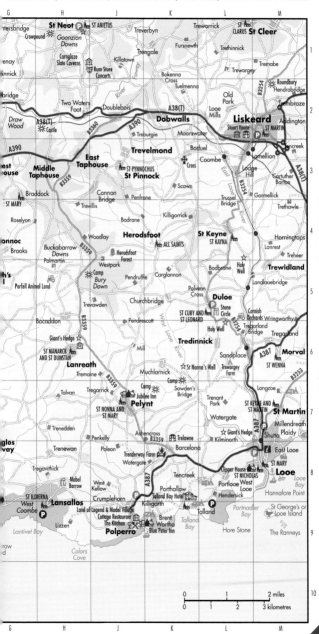

St Neot · ST ANIETUS · Treverbyn · Treworrick · St CLARUS · St Cleer

Crowpound · Goonzion Downs · Fursnewth · Trethinnick · Treworgey · Tremabe

Cannaglaze Slate Caverns · Killatown · Trengale · Roundbury · Hendrabridge

Rum Store Concerts · Bokenna Cross · Tuelmenna · Old Park · Looe Mills · Trembraze

Two Waters Foot · Doublebois · A38(T) · Liskeard · Abdington

Draw Wood · A38(T) · Castle · B3360 · A390 · Dobwalls · Stuart House · ST MARTIN · Bancreek

East Taphouse · Trebugie · Moorswater · Lamellion · Carthuther Barton

Middle Taphouse · Trevelmond · Boduel · Lodge Hill · Gormellick · Trethawle

Braddock · ST PYNNOCHUS · St Pinnock · Coombe · Cross · Scawn

ST MARY · Connon Bridge · Penfrane · Trussel Bridge

Roselyon · Trevillis · Bodrane · Killigorrick

Brooks · Buckabarrow Downs · Woodlay · Herodsfoot · ALL SAINTS · St Keyne · ST KAYNA · Horningtops

Polmartin · Westpark · Herodsfoot Forest · Bodbrane · Holy Well · Lanrest · Treheer

Parfell Animal Land · Camp Bury Down · Pendruffle · Carglannon · Polvean Cross · Trewidland · Landlooebridge

Trevawden · Churchbridge · Duloe · Stone Circle · Cornish Orchards · Wringworthy

Bocaddon · Pendrescott · ST CUBY AND ST LEONARD · Holy Well · Tregarland Bridge · Tregarland

Giant's Hedge · Mill · Tredinnick · Sandplace · Morval · ST WENNA

ST MANARCK AND ST DUNSTAN · Lanreath · St Norne's Well · Treworgey Farm · Longcoe

Tremaine · Muchlarnick · Camp · Sowden's Bridge · Trenant Park · ST KEYNE AND ST MARTIN · St Martin

Talvan · Tregarrick · Jubilee Inn · Pelynt · Watergate · Millendreath · Plaidy

ST NONNA & ST MARY · Giant's Hedge · Kilminarth · Shutta

Trenedden · Penkelly · Ashencross · B3359 · Trelawne · Barcelona · East Looe

Trenewan · Poleon · Tencreek · Clipper House · ST NICHOLAS · Looe

Tregavithick · Trenderway Farm · Watergate · Portloe · West Looe · Looe Bay

Mabel Barrow · West Kellow · Porthallow · Hendersick · Hannafore Point

ST ILDIERNA · Lansallos · Crumplehorn · Talland Bay Hotel · St George's or Looe Island

West Coombe · Lizzen · Land of Legend & Model Village · Killigarth · Portnadler Bay · The Ranneys

Lantivet Bay · Cottage Restaurant · The Kitchen · Polperro · Brent Wortha · Blue Peter Inn · Talland · Talland Bay · Hore Stone

Colors Cove

0   1   2 miles
0   1   2   3 kilometres

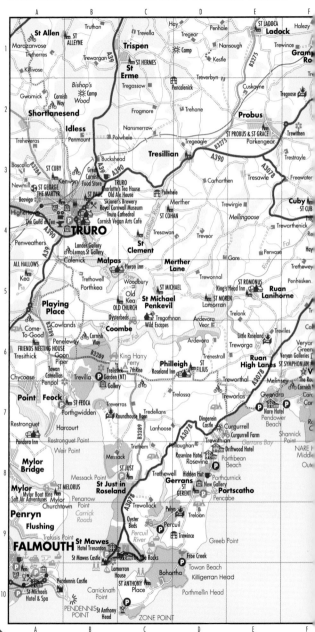

Coombe
Dowgas
Trelowth
Tregorrick
Duporth
Carrickowel Point
Polgooth
ST LEVAN
Porthpean
Downderry
A390
Hewas Water
Sticker
London Apprentice
Phoebe's Point
Garlenick
Lavalsa Meor
Ropehaven
Grampound
CROSS
Penans
B3287
Paramoor
Little Polgooth
Cornish Way
Lobb's Shop
Polstreath
Gerrans Point
Levalsa
Towan
Trenarren
The Bite
Rescorla
Nansladron
Polglaze
Hallane
Drennick
Black Head
Creed Gardens
ST ANDREW
Fair Cross
CROSS
Lower Barn
Tregian
Lanhadron
Pentewan
Gamas Point
Gargus
Pensagillies
Crosswyn
Cornish Way
Pentewan Beach
Mevagissey Bay
Pittsdown
St Ewe
ALL SAINTS
Crown Inn
Heligan Gardens
Portgiskey
Penare Point
Trevalsa Court Hotel
Polmassick
Treworrick
Beacon Cross
ST PETER
World of Model Railways
Mevagissey
Tregonan
Kestle
Folk Museum
Stuckumb Point
Trelissick
Penwarne
Portmellon
Shark
Tregarton
Tregerrick
Castle Hill
Bodrugan's Leap
Chapel Point
Trelucky
Trevarrick
High Lanes
Bodrugan Barton
Colona Beach
Turbot Point
The Veen
Gorran Churchtown
Castle
Pabyer Point
St Michael Caerhays
Caerhays Castle
Treveor
ST GORAN
Trewollock
Gwineas or Gwinges
Cornish Way
ST MICHAEL
Portholland
Boswinger
Gorran Haven
ST GORANUS
Tippet's Shop
Tretheake
Perbargus Point
Pen-a-maen or Maenease Point
Trahans
Tregenna
Greeb Point
Hemmick Beach
Penare
Bow or Vault Beach
Portloe
Caragloose Point
Veryan Bay
Penveor Point
Hartriza Point
High Point
Lizard Pool
Dodman Horse
Lugger Hotel
Manare Point
DODMAN POINT
Straythe
Blouth
Cove
Rock

0   1   2 miles
0   1   2   3 kilometres

103

THE LIZARD PENINSULA

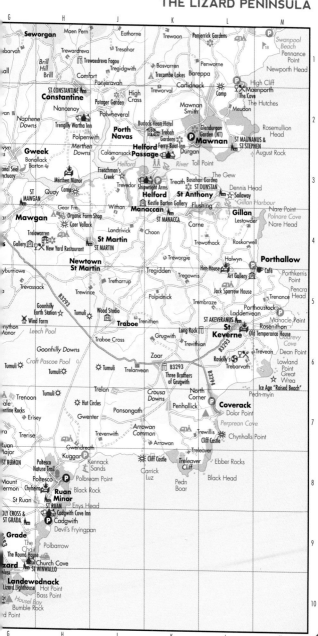

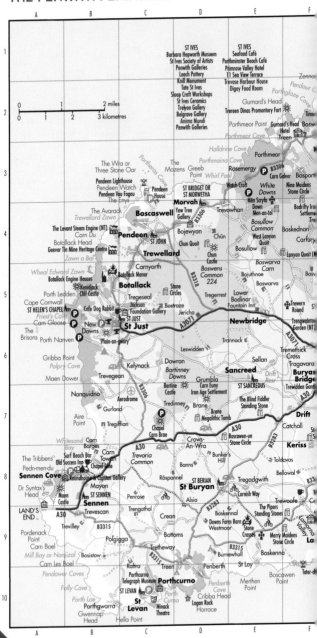

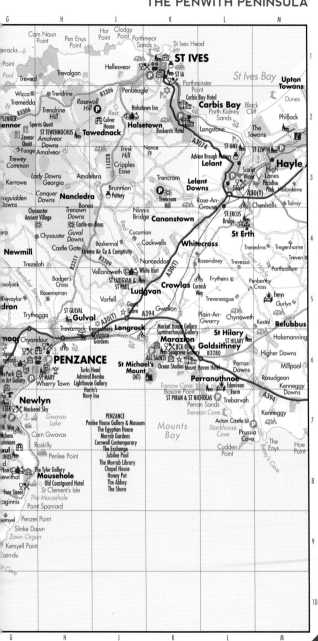

INDEX TO FEATURED ATTRACTIONS

A

Abbey Hotel 52
Adrian Brough Pottery 66
AK Wildlife Cruises 62
Altarnun 16
Althea House 40
Anima Mundi 64
Ann Thomas 66
Antony House & Gardens 56
Antony Woodland Garden 58
Arthurian Centre 76
Arts Café 30
Atlantic Surf Pods 42

B

Barbara Hepworth Museum 68
Barefoot Glamping 42
Beach Hut 28
Bedruthan Steps 18
Bedruthan Steps Hotel 38
Beside The Wave 64
BCK Bistro 30
Blue Hills Tin Streams 70
Blue Reef Aquarium 62
Boconnoc 36
Bodmin & Wenford Railway 72
Bodmin 4
Bodmin Jail 52
Bodmin Moor 60
Bodmin Museum 68
Bosahan Garden 58
Boscastle 12
Boscastle Harbour to Port Isaac 23
Boscastle's Farm Shop & Café 54
Bosvigo 58
Botallack Engine Houses 42
Bude 4
Bude to Boscastle Harbour 22
Bude's Old Canal 72
Budock Vean 38
Bugle to the Eden Project 76

C

Cadgwith 16
Caerhays Castle & Gardens 50
Caerhays Estate Luxury Holiday
Cottages 44
Café Dog & Rabbit 30
Callestock Cider Farm 39
Calstock 13
Calstock Viaduct 72
Camborne & Redruth 10
Camel Creek Adventure Park 76
Camel Trail 76
Camel Valley Vineyards 54
Carbis Bay Hotel 38
Cardinham Woods 76

Carew Arms 32
Carnglaze Slate Caverns 72
Carrick Roads 60
CAST 30
Castle-An-Dinas 50
Cawsand & Kingsand 10
Chapel House 36
Chapel Porth Surf Break 20
Charlestown 12
Chysauster Ancient Village 46
Circle Contemporary 64
Coast to Coast Trail 76
Combe Valley Nature Trail 60
Coombeshead Farm 40
Cornish Arms 32
Cornish Birds of Prey Centre 62
Cornish Gold & Pearl 72
Cornish Mines & Engines 33
Cornish Cyder Farm 54
Cornish Day Sailing 74
Cornish Tippi Holidays 42
Cornish Vegan 30
Cornwall Contemporary 64
Coswarth House 40
Cotehele House 56
Cotehele Quay 72
Coverack 16
Curgurrell Farm 54

D

Dairyland Farmworld 76
Daymer Bay 18
Delabole Slate Quarry 70
Digey Food Room 30
Dolcoath Mine 70
Driftwood Hotel 36
Duke of Cornwall's Light Infantry
Museum 68

E

East Pool Mine 56
Eden Project 58
Ednovean Farm 40
Ennys 44
Enys Gardens 58
Extreme Academy 74

F

Falmouth 4
Falmouth Art Gallery 68
Falmouth Pottery 66
Falmouth School of Sailing 74
Ferry Boat Inn 32
Fifteen Cornwall 28
Finley & Poppy Airstreams 42
Fistral 18
Fistral Beach Surf School 74
Fistral Surf Break 20